AF871668

ZEROES & ONES

Cristy Burne

First published in Xoum by Brio Books in 2018

Brio Books Pty Ltd
PO Box Q324, QVB Post Office,
NSW 1230, Australia
www.briobooks.com.au

Text copyright © Cristy Burne 2018
Design, illustration and typeset copyright © Brio Books 2018

ISBN 978-1-925589-39-9 (print)
ISBN 978-1-925589-40-5 (eBook)

This book is copyright. All rights reserved. Except under the conditions described in the Copyright Act 1968 (Aust) and subsequent amendments, and any exceptions permitted under the current statutory licence scheme administered by the Copyright Agency, no part of this publication may be reproduced, stored in a retrieval system, transmitted, broadcast or communicated in any form or by any means, optical, digital, electronic, scanning, mechanical, photocopying, recording or otherwise, without the prior written permission of both the copyright holders and the publisher.

The moral right of the author has been asserted.

Cataloguing-in-Publication data is available from the National Library of Australia

Cover design, text design and typesetting by Xou Creative, www.xou.com.au

Printed in China through Asia Pacific Offset Limited

Papers used by Brio Books are natural, recyclable products made from wood grown in sustainable forests. The manufacturing processes conform to the environmental regulations of the country of origin.

Part IV: Doing Social

Part V: Wrestling

Part II: Getting Personal

Part III: Going Global

Contents

For the innovators
of tomorrow

Hello
:-)

Hello world!

Digital technologies are changing the way we live and learn and connect. And they're changing fast.

Billions of ordinary people are connected to the internet. We use the web to trade money, ideas, insults and inspiration. We upload and download movies, information and cat videos. We can phone a friend, spam an enemy or play computer games with total strangers. And we can work as a team with people all over the world to solve global challenges.

This same enabling technology also makes us vulnerable to hackers, viruses, identity theft and cybercrime. And it also means we think of 'like', 'friend', and 'share' as clickable buttons.

How did our world come to be this way?

Who do we thank? Who should we blame?

And what will the next fifty years bring?

CompWHOter? CompYOUter

They spied and they stole.

They hatched ideas and built prototypes.

They were arrested, went broke, ate pizza and dreamed big.

And their achievements radically changed the way we live.

This book is about the creators of today's digital technologies. It's about the coders, the crackpots and the trailblazers. It's about their failure and despair, their dedication and daring.

But most of all, it's about what ordinary people can do with some creativity, determination, and a whole bunch of zeroes and ones. People like you.

Back in time

Just fifty years ago, there was no such thing as email. Or wi-fi. Or the internet.

There were no smartphones, no game consoles, no digital cameras.

Computers were the size of houses. Data was stored on magnetic tape. Phones were connected to your wall with a springy cord. Music was stored on discs you collected until they filled your entire bedroom.

Some people thought this was the pinnacle of technological innovation. They were wrong.

'People will soon get tired of staring at a plywood box every night.' **Darryl F Zanuck, executive at 20th Century Fox, on the future of TV, 1946**

'Remote shopping, while entirely feasible, will flop.' ***Time Magazine*, 1966**

'There is no reason for any individual to have a computer in his home.' **Ken Olsen, founder of Digital Equipment Corporation, 1977**

'I predict the Internet will soon go spectacularly supernova and in 1996 catastrophically collapse.' **Robert Metcalfe*, founder of 3Com and co-inventor of Ethernet, 1995**

'The truth is no online database will replace your daily newspaper, no CD-ROM can take the place of a competent teacher and no computer network will change the way government works.' **Clifford Stoll, for *Newsweek*, 1995**

'There's just not that many videos I want to watch.' **Steve Chen, co-founder of YouTube expressing concerns about his company's long-term viability, 2005**

'Everyone's always asking me when Apple will come out with a cell phone. My answer is, "Probably never."' **David Pogue, *The New York Times* blog, 2006**

*Just two years later, Robert literally ate his own words: he printed them out, popped them in a blender, and then munched them right up.

Two BILLION computers … and counting!

There are more than two billion personal computers on our planet.

If you used each computer for just one second, it would take more than sixty years to use them all. And you wouldn't have even started on the squillions of other devices: tablets, smartphones, game consoles and more.

But not so long ago, there were no computers in the entire world. Zero. Zilch. Zip.

This is COLOSSAL!

In the 1940s, one of the first programmable electronic computers—nicknamed Colossus, which means enormous and hugely powerful—contained around 1500 switches.

That might sound like a colossal number, but today you can fit billions of switches on a chip small enough to wear on your wrist.

And tomorrow? Who knows? Perhaps you can help to create the future.

Meet the revolutionaries

Digital technologies are developed by regular people: people like you and me (and even the person sitting next to you!). It's up to all of us to imagine—and create—our best tomorrows.

To understand the future, let's take a look at the past.

This book takes us back to see where it all began ... So sit back, relax and enjoy the non-digital ride. Hope you packed some pizza!

PART ONE
KICKING OFF

1800s on: Cow-catchers, party tricks and Flyology

Two hundred years ago, you'd bathe once a week if you were lucky, and there was no such thing as a shower. Doctors thought bad smells caused disease, and that harvesting your blood cured it. And if you so much as stole a loaf of bread in England, you'd be shipped off to Australia as a convict. Life was tough. Plus, there was no Google. No TV. No telephone. Not even radio had been invented.

That didn't stop clever inventors from imagining the future of computing. Today it's hard to believe that their predictions could be so spot on.

The tech: The Difference Engine (never finished) and the Analytical Engine (never started)
Thought up by: Charles Babbage and Ada Lovelace

Ada! Sole daughter of my house and of my heart!

Born in 1815, Ada Lovelace was the daughter of famous poet and nonstop party animal, Lord Byron.

But Ada's mum, Lady Byron, didn't dig nonstop partying. In fact, Lord Byron was such a load of trouble, she and Ada moved out when Ada was just a teensy baby.

You see, Ada's mum was a sensible mathematician. And she didn't want Ada to end up like her troublesome dad.

Diagnosis? High risk of poetic party brain (AKA madness). Prescription? Maths. Lots of maths. Studying maths will quash any fanciful tendencies, surely ... Lady Byron, probably

Fortunately for us, Lady Byron's plan backfired*. The more maths Ada studied, the more her imagination grew.

***But we love her anyway. Two hundred years ago, maths wasn't something most young ladies were encouraged to study. But thanks to Lady Byron (and a whole bunch of tutors), Ada's mathe-magical mind went on to change the world.**

Let's get this party started, LB's in the house!

The Discovering Faculty

When Ada was twelve, she began a new project: she spent hours trying to learn how to fly. She even wrote a book on her findings. She called it *Flyology*. Her research convinced her there was a strong link between imagination and science.

'What is imagination? ... Imagination is the Discovering Faculty ... It is that which penetrates into the unseen worlds around us, the worlds of Science.' Ada Lovelace

The name's Babbage*

Charles Babbage was born on Boxing Day in 1791. He trained as a mathematician and engineer, practised as an inventor and (like Lord Byron) he loved to party. Charles would invite loads of lords and ladies—plus explorers, writers, actors and scientists—to his place. Then they'd all eat, drink, dance, romance, and hopefully swoon over his latest projects.

My awesome projects, by Charles

- cow-catcher (for protecting trains)
- flashing lighthouse signals (for coded communication with ships)
- tidal power (for when coal runs out) (Note to self: must get started on this, pronto!)
- disaster recorder (for railway crashes)
- dynamometer car (for measuring how well a train engine performs)
- theatre lights with coloured filters for that killer party atmosphere (Whoops: the theatre manager fears my lights will burst into flames; I have reassured him, and arranged for two fire engines to be on stage, just in case) (Nope. Still not allowed. My genius goes unappreciated, again!)
- tic-tac-toe machine for ... not sure yet. (Idea: what if I charge people to play it and make millions!)
- ophthalmoscope (for checking out what's inside the human eye)
- difference engine for adding up numbers (I think this one's my fave!)

*(rhymes with cabbage)

Party trick

When Ada was seventeen, she went to one of Charles' parties. She wasn't so keen on dancing and romancing, but her mathematical brain fell in love with Charles' projects. He'd built a small section of the Difference Engine, and when he showed her how it could spit out answers to maths questions, she was thrilled. Dozens of cogs. Discs and shafts. And you could work the whole machine just by winding a giant arm. It was technology at the cutting edge.

Ada scooted home to write a letter to Charles. She told him how totally splendid his invention was. He wrote back, telling her how straight-up epic her maths was. And that was that: science at first sight. The pair kept writing to each other, and bouncing ideas around, for nearly twenty years.

'I have a peculiar way of learning, and I think it must be a peculiar man to teach me successfully.'
Ada Lovelace to Charles Babbage

Playing with numbers

Charles' mechanical designs set Ada's fantastic brain into action. She began to wonder whether Charles' machines might be able to do more than just maths. She dared to dream that machines might one day use numbers as a code, allowing them to reach beyond maths into literature, music and art.

'The engine can arrange and combine its numerical quantities exactly as if they were letters or any other general symbols ...' Ada Lovelace

'The engine might compose elaborate and scientific pieces of music of any degree of complexity or extent.' Ada Lovelace

This idea was super-duper out there for the 1800s. But, just as Ada predicted, some of today's most advanced artificially intelligent computers are indeed composing their own music.

Countin' Countess

Ada's mum's cousin ended up becoming Britain's Prime Minister, which meant Ada was in luck. The new PM was advisor to Queen Victoria, and the Queen soon made Ada's husband an earl, and Ada a countess. So now that's Lady Lovelace to you, peasant.

Jacquard's loom

Before Ada was even born, modern computing received a kick up the woven pants: Joseph Marie Jacquard invented the automatic loom.

Looms are used to weave complicated patterns into fabric. Joseph Marie's loom could weave a pattern automatically. It used bits of cardboard with holes punched into it as a way of controlling the loom. If the card had a hole in it, a thread could go through. If there was no hole, there was no thread. Each row of the pattern was encoded using a different card.

So, by coding the position of the holes, you could program the loom to automatically create a pattern.

When Babbage saw these punch cards, a not-yet-invented

lightbulb went off in his head. He realised the cards might be used for other patterns, too. And the rest, as they say, is computing history.

The Analytical Engine

Charles' design for the Analytical Engine was part science, part science-fiction. He imagined it would perform calculations. It would store numbers in a separate memory. You could even program it, just by punching a series of coded holes into cardboard.

Unfortunately, the Analytical Engine was never built. Charles ran out of money, and the government stopped funding his incredibly expensive (you want *how much*!?!?), massively ambitious (you're planning to do *what*?!?!) engine experiments.

Notes by the translator

In 1843, Ada did a little job for Charles. An Italian engineer named Luigi Menabrea* had written an 8000-word essay about the Analytical Engine. Trouble was, it was written entirely in French.

So clever Ada translated Luigi's words into English. Along the way, she added more than 19,000 mega-clever words of her own. In these 'Notes', Ada describes how she would program Charles' Analytical Engine to calculate Bernoulli numbers.**

'The notes of the Countess of Lovelace extend to about three times the length of the original

memoir. Their author has entered fully into almost all the very difficult and abstract questions connected with the subject.' Charles Babbage

Ada's 'Notes' are often credited as including the first computer program, and the first use of subroutines (mini-codes that can be used over and over again).

'A new, a vast, and a powerful language is developed for the future use of analysis.' Ada Lovelace

*Luigi went on to become the seventh Prime Minister of Italy.
**Bernoulli numbers are useful to people who study pure mathematics for fun. Yes, such people exist.

Luigi Menabrea,
Italian engineer and PM.

Bernoulli numbers

So just how clever was Ada? And why did she need such a massive machine to count a few measly numbers? Good questions. After all, calculating Bernoulli numbers is sooooo easy. Here is an example formula:

$$B_m = \sum_{k=0}^{m} \sum_{v=0}^{k} (-1)^v \binom{k}{v} \frac{v^m}{k+1}$$

$$B_m^+ = \sum_{k=0}^{m} \sum_{v=0}^{k} (-1)^v \binom{k}{v} \frac{(v+1)^m}{k+1}$$

Bernoulli. Rhymes with truly and unruly.

And, of course, these are some of the answers ...

n	0	1	2	4	6	8	
B_n	1	$-\frac{1}{2}$	$\frac{1}{6}$	$-\frac{1}{30}$	$\frac{1}{42}$	$-\frac{1}{30}$	*(continued below)*

n	10	12	14	16	18	20	
B_n	$\frac{1}{66}$	$-\frac{691}{2730}$	$\frac{7}{6}$	$-\frac{3617}{510}$	$\frac{43869}{798}$	$-\frac{174611}{330}$	*(it keeps going)*

If you're having trouble, don't worry. So am I. But it does show how brilliant these early innovators were.

So how did they work out such a complicated problem? They broke each enormous mathematical problem into many smaller problems. In this way, they could work out a hugely complicated equation by following a series of easy steps.

So if a person could work out the maths, surely that person could also teach a machine to do the maths for them.

Cool fact: this Japanese guy, Seki Takakazu, independently found the numbers at around the same time as Bernoulli.

Into the future

When people began to build the world's first computers, they built on Charles and Ada's ideas. Even today, hundreds of years after Charles and Ada's deaths, their notes, designs and dreams live on.

In 1985, enthusiasts from London's Science Museum built Charles' Difference Engine to his exact design.

What would you do?

- Do you think maths is an antidote to creativity? Why? Why not?
- Some people don't believe Ada was the author of her 'Notes'. They say she was delusional and pretended to be smarter than she was. Other people say this is poppycock, and that Ada understood the future of computing even better than Charles. Why do you think these two arguments exist? What makes Ada's achievements so amazing for their time?
- One of Ada's tutors was a mathematician called Mary Somerville. Mary was one of the few female mathematicians around in the 1800s. Do you think it's important to have the help of someone who has experienced what you're going through? What happens when you're the very first?
- Every year we celebrate Ada's work on Ada Lovelace Day: the second Tuesday in October. There's also a programming language, Ada, named after her. Charles Babbage also has a programming language named after him, and a moon crater, too. Can you imagine some other ways we might celebrate and remember Ada and Charles' work?

1906 on: Race tracks, fast money and a railroad engineer

Imagine a computer made of clock parts and held together with bicycle chain and miles of flexible wiring. Now use it to get mega-rich. Hello, ingenuity.

The tech: The Julius tote: a large-scale, multi-user, real-time data processing system, also known as the automatic totalisator
Invented by: George Julius

Loco-motion

As a kid, George Julius loved helping his dad to fix clocks. Aged seventeen, he put his mechanical mind to good use, studying engineering at the University of New Zealand (UNZ)*.

George became UNZ's first graduate with a speciality in railway engineering. He soon nabbed a job as assistant engineer for the Western Australian Government Railways Locomotive Department.

***George was at UNZ with Ernest Rutherford, the chap who split the atom and won the 1908 Nobel Prize for Chemistry.**

Meanwhile, at the racing track ...

Totalisators—or totes—were used at racing tracks to take and total the bets that people placed on which horse would win each race. You had to queue up to place your bet, waiting while a human struggled to keep count and calculate your betting odds. So. Slow.

Totes for democracy

George never intended to invent a computer for placing bets. In fact, his first plan was political, and inspired by a mate:

'A friend in the west conceived the idea of getting me to make a machine to register votes, and so to expedite elections by giving the result without any human intervention.' George Julius

Nice one, thought George. He set about inventing such a machine, then sent it to the government.

They rejected his idea. Fail.

But the racing industry loved it. Ka-ching!

'Up to that time I had never seen a racecourse. A friend ... explained to me what was required in an efficient totalisator. I found the problem of great interest as the perfect tote must have a mechanism capable of adding the records from a number of operators all of whom might issue a ticket on the same horse at the same instant. I set to work on a machine that would permit the simultaneous addition, give instantaneous records, and would satisfy the requirements of any racecourse.' George Julius

George and his kids built a prototype tote in their back shed.

Turbo gambling, at your service

George's tote was faster. Much. Faster. Soon gamblers could lose money quicker than ever before.

The Julius tote could:

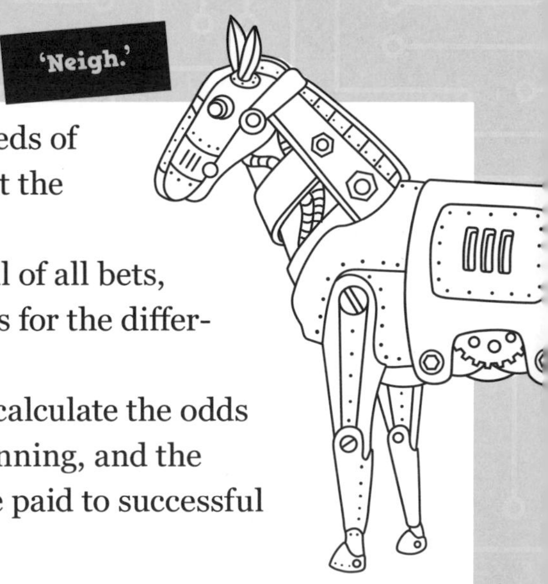

- accept bets from hundreds of different gamblers, all at the same time
- add up the running total of all bets, including separate totals for the different horses in a race
- use the totalled bets to calculate the odds of a particular horse winning, and the dividends that would be paid to successful punters.

Today, these tasks are done by software engineers with the latest and greatest in modern computing and electronics. Back then, George did it with wheels and cogs. The early Julius totes were around 10 × 10 metres, or the size of a small house.

'Although it looked like a giant tangle of piano wires, pulleys and cast iron boxes and many racing officials predicted that it would not work, it was a great success.' Brian Conlon, an engineer in George's company

It's a winner!

George's dad hated betting, but that didn't stop George's invention becoming an instant hit around the globe. His first tote was installed in 1913 at the Ellerslie Park Racecourse, in New Zealand, and could take thirty bets at a time. The second was installed at the Gloucester Park racetrack in Western Australia, with eighty-six different windows to take bets.

The Julius tote in Longchamps, France, could take 273 bets at a time; the one in White City, London, could do 320. Test

totes built in Sydney could take 1000 bets at a time, selling up to 250,000 bets in just one minute.

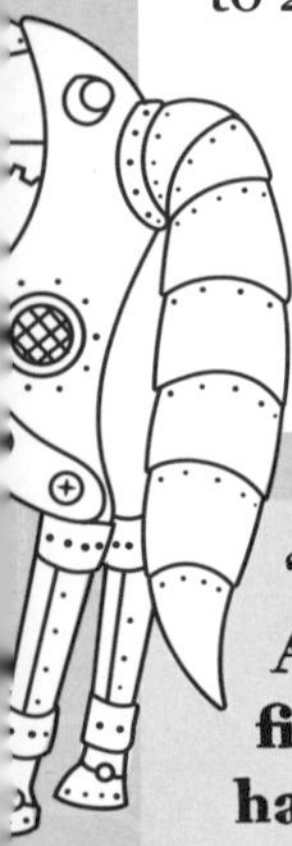

George's company went on to sell the Julius totes into nearly thirty countries. They even made money during the Great Depression, when loads of other companies went broke.

'I have pleasure in stating that the "Premier" Automatic Totalisator Machines ... which were first used at the Club's Spring Meeting, 1917, have, since their installation, given complete satisfaction. Their accuracy is unquestionable and the rapidity with which tickets are issued by the experienced operators leaves nothing to be desired.' Australian Jockey Club, 1922

Don't I know you from somewhere?

As well as inventing the tote and smashing the tote market for decades, George was also:

- the first chairman of Australia's famous Commonwealth Scientific and Industrial Research Organisation, or CSIRO (back then it was the plain old CSIR)
- knighted by King George V in 1929
- the son of New Zealand's first Archbishop
- married to Eva O'Connor, the daughter of engineer CY O'Connor (who built the famous Kalgoorlie–Perth pipeline)
- the dad of the 'likeable, charming' and infamous burglar Gentleman George, who broke into houses

to steal stuff (including lawnmowers), but made sure everything was clean and tidy when he left. Aw, thanks George Jnr!

Into the future

In 1925, fourteen-year-old David Myers was in the audience when George gave a talk about his tote.

David was fascinated by what he heard. He went on to study science and engineering at uni, and worked for CSIR, just like George. Years later, David invented CSIRO's Differential Analyser, one of Australia's most famous computers.

What would you do?

- **George built his computer to help with government elections. How do you think he felt when the government rejected his invention? What do you imagine he did next? What would you have done?**
- **George helped his dad fix clocks, and George's kids helped him invent the tote. How can kids best contribute when they work with adults in a team? What project would you like to work on? Who would you have on your team?**
- **What do you think are some of the reasons the government decided to stick with paper votes, and not adopt George's invention to allow electronic voting?**
- **What features would you include on your own electronic voting machine?**

1937 on: Lightbulb moments, kitchen antics and binary, baby

For centuries a 'computer' was someone who helped work out maths problems. But things really started moving in computer land when we worked out what made a great computing machine.

The tech: All kinds of experimental computing machines
Invented by: A whole bunch of people, almost at the same time

Things get kinda busy

In 1937, the computing machine scene was really getting hot. Here's how things went down:

- A circus-obsessed student at MIT named Claude Shannon put down his juggling pins and unicycle long enough to work out that you could use electrical circuits to represent logic. Much later, Claude went on to invent a Rubik's Cube solver, a juggling machine, a flame-throwing trumpet and a robotic mouse that could learn (and remember) its way through a maze. But his most important invention was that key idea: that computers could use electric circuits.
- A mathematician called George Stibitz read Claude's idea. He built a demonstration circuit in his kitchen, using lightbulbs and a switch he made from an old tobacco tin. He engineered a lit lightbulb to mean '1' and an unlit bulb to mean '0'. He named his invention Model K (for kitchen). By 1939 he'd finished a much bigger version.
- A high-school-dropout-turned-Harvard-student named Howard Aiken climbed into a dusty university attic and found a few broken bits of some-guy-called-Charles-Babbage's Difference Engine. First, Howard went *Huh?* then he went *Nice! Let's build ourselves a bigger-and-better version*. And so Howard and the folks at Harvard did just that. They called it Mark I.
- Meanwhile, an inventor called John Vincent Atanasoff was building his own computer in his basement. He used vacuum tubes as switches and rotating drums to store data, and he also used a binary on–off logic system. But when John was called away to serve in

World War II, his computer was left to gather dust. Years later, it was destroyed for its parts.

- On the other side of the Atlantic, a German engineer named Konrad Zuse was experimenting in his parents' apartment. He built an electromechanical computer called the Z1. Then he built a Z2. And a Z3. But all three models were blown up when the Allies bombed Berlin in World War II.
- Also, around 1937 a chap named John Mauchly was thinking he'd like to build a computer too ...

Into the mix

In 1940, John Mauchly saw a demonstration of George Stibitz's latest computer. In 1941, he visited John Atanasoff's basement, to see his computer. And he saw MIT's new computer too.

And then he met J Presper Eckert, nicknamed Pres. Together, John and Pres hatched a plan to build a computer that would combine the best of everything ...

ID File: Pres Eckert

- **Wealthy:** The only son of a millionaire.
- **Inventor:** As a kid, Pres built a system for steering model boats, and an electrical intercom.
- **Entrepreneur:** At school Pres made money by building radios for his friends.
- **Joker:** While still at school, Pres created the Osculometer: a machine that measured the passion of a kiss by the sweatiness of the kisser.

Decimal, dude

You probably have ten toes. Take some time to check ... Done already? You speedy thing! But because you have ten toes, it's pretty easy for us to count to ten. Same goes with fingers. Which is probably why most of the world counts using a base-10 or 'decimal' system.

In a base-10 system, you use ten digits to represent numbers: 0, 1, 2, 3, 4, 5, 6, 7, 8 and 9.

The value of each digit changes depending on where it is in the number. In the decimal system, numbers can be in the ones (1), tens (10), hundreds (10 × 10), thousands (10 × 10 × 10), ten thousands (10 × 10 × 10 × 10), or hundred thousands (10 × 10 × 10 × 10 × 10) place, and so on.

Base-10 quiz:

How many days in a week?
7 = (7 × 1)
And how many days in a year?
365 = (3 × 100) + (6 × 10) + (5 × 1)
Too easy. You are truly a base-10 master.

Binary, baby

Tragically, computers don't have toes. Take some time to check ... Done already? Told you so.

In the absence of toes, computers must rely on something else to help them count. They use on–off switches. Which is why modern computers use a base-2 or 'binary' system.

0 = off and 1 = on

In a base-2 system, numbers can be in the ones (1), twos (2), fours (2 × 2), eights (2 × 2 × 2), sixteens (2 × 2 × 2 × 2) or thirty-twos (2 × 2 × 2 × 2 × 2) place, and so on.

Base-2 quiz

How many days in a week? 111 = (1 × 4) + (1 × 2) + (1 × 1)
And how many days in a year? 101101101 = (1 × 256) + (0 × 128) + (1 × 64) + (1 × 32) + (0 × 16) + (1 × 8) + (1 × 4) + (0 × 2) + (1 × 1)
If you're not used to working in binary, base-2 can blow your mind. But for computers, it's the simplest maths there is.

Analogue to digital

The real world is analogue: things happen along a continuous scale. An analogue clock, for example, measures time using hands that can point anywhere on the clock's dial.

In a digital world, things are different. A digital clock divides time into minutes and seconds. Colours are divided into black or white. Answers can be yes or no. There are no in-betweens.

And digital computers are the same: they work by dividing continuous analogue signals into on–off signals.

Into the future

You can tell your computer is modern if it fits these four criteria:

- **Electronic.** No bicycle wheels or click-clacking levers. Electronic computing relies on electrical signals, which

can move at nearly the speed of light. BAM! You've outpaced the click-clacking competition by millions of operations per second.

- **Digital.** In a digital world, things are either black or white, on or off, up or down, zero or one. Just like in a computer switch. There's no room for in-between.*
- **Binary.** Forget trying to make a ten-way switch to allow for base-10 maths. Everything your computer does is coded into base-2: 0s and 1s, all the way.
- **Programmable.** Gone are the days when your computer could only perform one type of equation, or play one type of game. Modern computers can follow programs that allow them to do a huge variety of things—and all without changing a wire.

*Analogue, on the other hand, is a sliding scale: You can be on, partly on, sort-of on, pretty-much on, totally on, or a smidgen, tad, tittle, jot, sliver or flyspeck on. And the same goes for off.

What would you do?

- John Mauchly and Pres Eckert invented their computer using ideas and information they'd gathered from seeing other people's computers. Do you think this is fair? Is this sort of thing restricted to computing? Where else does it happen?
- The year 1937 was a busy one for computing, and then in 1939, World War II began. Over the next few years, the modern computer was born. Many of the world's largest jumps in technology have come during times of war. Why do you think this is?

During World War II, mathematicians—otherwise known as human computers—were an essential part of the Allies' war effort. Even so, these walking whizzes were soon replaced with digital computers. But those giant machines couldn't program themselves. Six of the US Army's best human computers were recruited for a secret mission: become digital programmers, and fast.

The tech: The 27-tonne giant, ENIAC (almost rhymes with maniac); probably the world's first fully electronic, programmable digital computer

Programmed by: The ENIAC Six: Jean Jennings Bartik, Frances 'Betty' Snyder Holberton, Marlyn Wescoff Meltzer, Kathleen 'Kay' McNulty Mauchly Antonelli, Frances Bilas Spence and Ruth Lichterman Teitelbaum

Ready, aim, fire!

Before they programmed computers, the ENIAC Six were human computers for the US Army.

While World War II raged, they used maths to predict the pathways of shells* being fired from cannons and guns. Using a pen and paper, these human computers calculated firing tables for each size of gun.

Each firing table listed around 1800 possible pathways for an explosive shell

×

Around 30 hours to hand-calculate one pathway

=

Around 54,000 hours of maths to complete one firing table. That's the equivalent of one person's brain calculating day and night without stopping for six years!

***Not shells as in seashells, but shells as in 100-kilo exploding bullets.**

Where's the shell gonna go?

To predict the pathyway of a shell, you will need:

- a pencil (hopefully with a massive eraser)
- a sheet of paper (preferably longer than yourself)
- the top speed of a speeding explosive, plus data on wind speed and direction, air resistance, curvature and rotation of the Earth, and more.

Remember: human computers were accurate to ten decimal places. On your marks, get set, go!

Five-minute maths break

In 1946, *Popular Science* magazine guessed a human computer could hand-calculate the following equation in five minutes. Want to give it a try?

$$2{,}156{,}789{,}463 \times 1{,}987{,}437{,}846 = 4{,}286{,}485{,}004{,}620{,}216{,}698$$

Need a calculator?

Some human computers were lucky. They had access to a mechanical calculator. These early calculators were around the size of a room and relied on cogs, gear wheels and levers. Not exactly pocket-sized.

There were only around six such calculators in the world, but they were popular. By using a mechanical calculator, a human computer could complete a pathway calculation in less than an hour.

Just one teensy problem: The calculator didn't always give the right answer. Not to worry. Human computers were also used to double-check the calculator's answers.

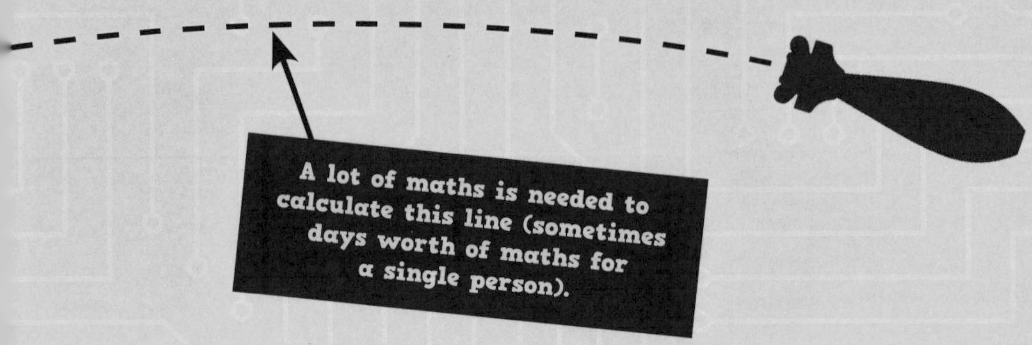

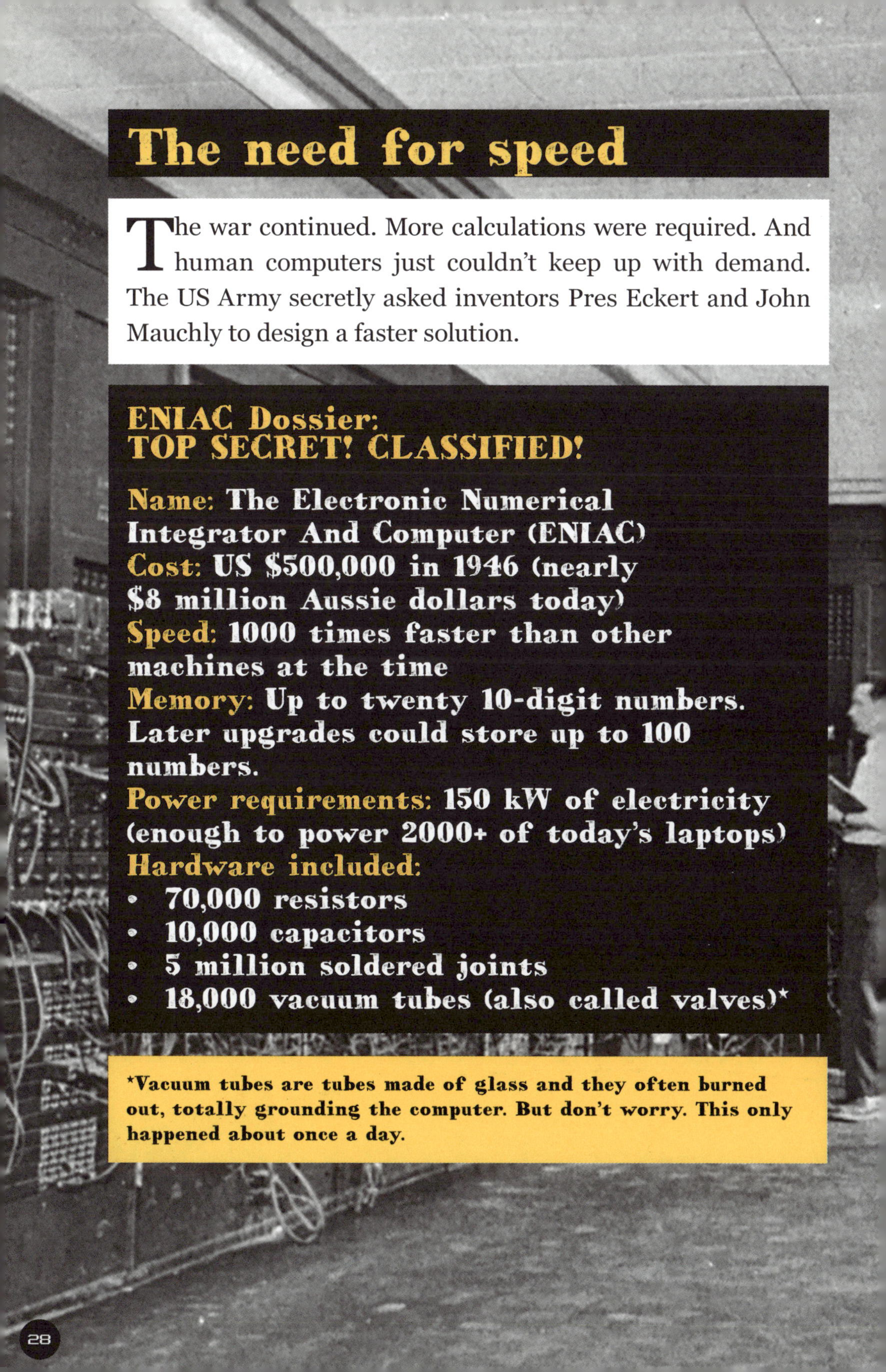

The need for speed

The war continued. More calculations were required. And human computers just couldn't keep up with demand. The US Army secretly asked inventors Pres Eckert and John Mauchly to design a faster solution.

ENIAC Dossier: TOP SECRET! CLASSIFIED!

Name: The Electronic Numerical Integrator And Computer (ENIAC)
Cost: US $500,000 in 1946 (nearly $8 million Aussie dollars today)
Speed: 1000 times faster than other machines at the time
Memory: Up to twenty 10-digit numbers. Later upgrades could store up to 100 numbers.
Power requirements: 150 kW of electricity (enough to power 2000+ of today's laptops)
Hardware included:

- 70,000 resistors
- 10,000 capacitors
- 5 million soldered joints
- 18,000 vacuum tubes (also called valves)*

*Vacuum tubes are tubes made of glass and they often burned out, totally grounding the computer. But don't worry. This only happened about once a day.

Behind closed doors

ENIAC was so new, it didn't come with instructions. And it was so secret, even the programmers weren't allowed to see it until after they'd written their first program.

'Someone gave us a whole stack of blueprints ... They said, "Here, you can figure out how the machine works, and then figure out how to program it." This was a little bit hard to do.' Kay McNulty

ENIAC wasn't programmed with a keyboard. The Six had to connect its tangle of plugs and switches into intricate order using miles of wires. Each program had to be connected in a different way. They'd work for days with pen and paper to create a single program. Then, it took hours to plug the program in.

Once programmed, ENIAC could calculate:

- 5000 additions or subtractions per second
- 350 multiplications per second
- 35 divisions per second (but seriously, who likes division anyway?).

This person in the photo is Betty Snyder of the ENIAC Six.

Faster than a speeding bullet

In its first public demonstration, ENIAC took just twenty seconds to calculate where a fired shell would land. It displayed the answer ten seconds before the shell landed.

'The day ENIAC was introduced to the world was one of the most exciting days of my life.' Jean Bartik

Into the future

The ENIAC Six kept programming computers and designing software for many years. They've all entered the Women in Technology International Hall of Fame.

'I had a lot of fun working on that machine, just an absolutely wonderful time.' Kay McNulty

What would you do?

- ENIAC may well have been the world's first digital computer, but did it have the world's best name? The acronym 'ENIAC' stood for 'Electronic Numerical Integrator And Computer'. Later computers were called EDVAC, ILLIAC and JOHNNIAC. What do you think these acronyms stood for? If you were naming a computer, what acronym would you use?
- The evening after ENIAC's first public demonstration, scientists, army personnel and ENIAC's inventors went out for a celebratory dinner. But ENIAC's female programmers weren't invited, recognised or even thanked. Why do you think this was? Do you think this attitude is changing?
- On ENIAC's fiftieth anniversary, some fans rebuilt the massive computer on a single microchip. What changes do you foresee in the next fifty years? Do you think things are still changing this quickly?

1949 on: CSIRAC, Colonel Bogey and a Melbourne Cup winner

Back when there was just a handful of computers in the world, the idea of using a valuable maths machine to play pop music was radical. And we Aussies certainly didn't build our first computers with the aim of making music. It just sort of turned out that way ...

The tech: Australia's first digital computers
Used by: Everyone who was anyone in Australian engineering and physics

Photo: CSIRO, 1952 (that's Trev in the picture, BTW)

To Australia, and beyond!

When Trevor Pearcey moved to Australia after World War II, there were fewer than five digital computers in the world. But Trev thought they were way cool, so he convinced the Council for Scientific and Industrial Research (CSIR, now CSIRO; pronounced 'sigh-row' by the cool kids) that Australia needed a digital computer of its own.

'Great idea,' we said.

We called our computer the CSIR Mark I, and designed and built it ourselves. CSIR Mark I was eventually renamed CSIRAC: CSIR's Automatic Computer (pronounced 'sigh-rack').

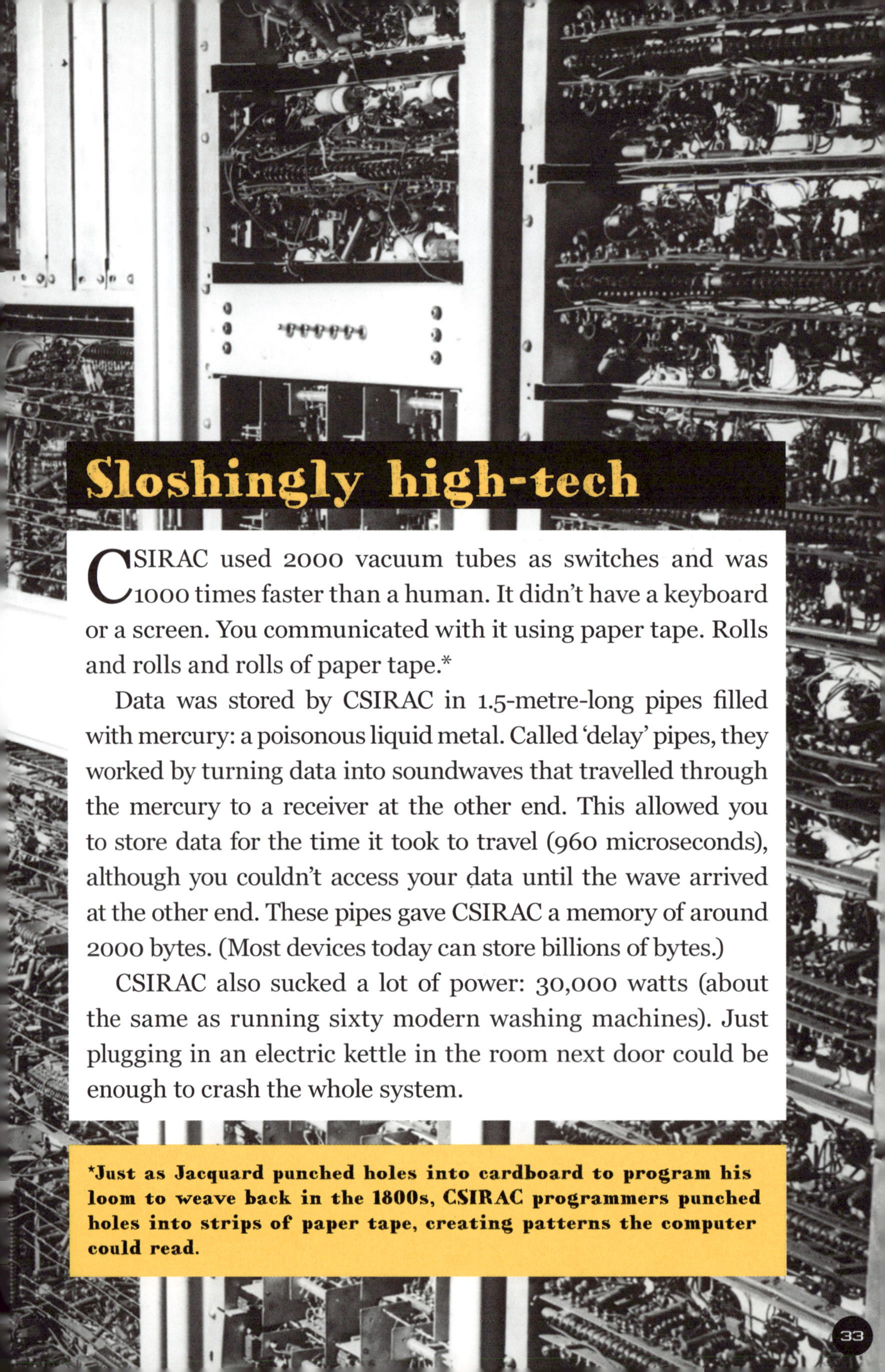

Sloshingly high-tech

CSIRAC used 2000 vacuum tubes as switches and was 1000 times faster than a human. It didn't have a keyboard or a screen. You communicated with it using paper tape. Rolls and rolls and rolls of paper tape.*

Data was stored by CSIRAC in 1.5-metre-long pipes filled with mercury: a poisonous liquid metal. Called 'delay' pipes, they worked by turning data into soundwaves that travelled through the mercury to a receiver at the other end. This allowed you to store data for the time it took to travel (960 microseconds), although you couldn't access your data until the wave arrived at the other end. These pipes gave CSIRAC a memory of around 2000 bytes. (Most devices today can store billions of bytes.)

CSIRAC also sucked a lot of power: 30,000 watts (about the same as running sixty modern washing machines). Just plugging in an electric kettle in the room next door could be enough to crash the whole system.

***Just as Jacquard punched holes into cardboard to program his loom to weave back in the 1800s, CSIRAC programmers punched holes into strips of paper tape, creating patterns the computer could read.**

The World Wide Woah?

Decades before the web was born, Trev was already thinking well into the future ...

'It is not inconceivable that an automatic encyclopaedic service operated through the national teleprinter or telephone service will one day exist.' Trevor Pearcey

Sing it to me, baby

For a long while, computers were used to calculate maths, but not for much else—especially not something as frivolous as playing music.

But mathematician Geoff Hill loved music, plus his mum and sister were music teachers. So, around 1950, CSIRAC is thought to have played the world's first digital computer music.

CSIRAC had a hooter that hooted when it reached certain points in its program. Geoff used this hooter and his perfect pitch to program the computer to play songs like 'Colonel Bogey', 'Bonnie Banks' and 'Girl with Flaxen Hair'. He could change the pitch of the hooter by controlling the time at which programmed instructions arrived.

Unfortunately there are no recordings of CSIRAC's music because it was supposed to be used for serious stuff, not mucking around.

Now, we make and listen to music on electronic devices every day. And it was an Australian who rocked out first.

The real work

CSIRAC's musical career was continued by programmer Thomas Cherry, who created a way for anyone to teach CSIRAC a new tune.

When it wasn't playing music, CSIRAC contributed to hundreds of important projects, including star gazing, weather forecasting, loan calculating and electricity supply.

Don't be SILLIAC

Australia's second computer was named SILLIAC, short for Sydney's ILLAIC (or Sydney's Illinois Automatic Computer).

SILLIAC was built because of a race. Optician and jeweller Adolph Basser owned a racehorse named Delta. When Adolph bet on Delta in the 1951 Melbourne Cup, Delta won!

Adolph donated his winnings—50,000 pounds, or around two million dollars today—to the SILLIAC project. (He also donated another 50,000 pounds later on, as well as funding a hospital, a library and a research institute. Way to go, Adolph!)

SILLIAC was soon busy twenty-four hours a day, seven days a week. Schools visited it, businesses used it, and more than 2000 of Australia's early engineers and researchers learned how to operate it.

'Everyone was aware that Sydney University and the Sydney University School of Physics had a computer, which nobody else had even heard of basically in those days.' Ian Johnston, a student at Sydney University at the time

The all-new compu-fridge!

SILLIAC was so big, it needed its own air-conditioning. The team thought this was terrific, and used the aircon's cooling ducts to keep their drinks cold.

From beginning to funeral march

When Sydney University decided to show its computer to the world, nine-year-old Jenny Edwards was there. At a university open day in 1956, Jenny played noughts and crosses against SILLIAC, and she won. She went on to study computing.

'I thought that was very exciting, and maybe it has sowed the seeds of my future career, although I didn't think very much about it at the time.' Jenny Edwards

At SILLIAC's retirement party in 1968, Jenny helped program the machine to play its own farewell music: five different versions of the funeral march.

'It taught us a lot of really good skills ... You had to do all kinds of interesting things to get it to make music.' Jenny Edwards

Into the future

After its retirement, CSIRAC was rescued from Death By Rubbish Bin and donated to the Applied Science Museum of Victoria. In 2018, it's at the Melbourne Museum and one of the oldest intact computers.

SILLIAC wasn't so lucky. It was taken to bits, and chunks of it were donated to universities, museums and fourteen computer-crazy kids. (It's true. I'm not just being SILLIAC.)

What would you do?

- In the early days of IT, people didn't understand what computers could do, or how they might be useful. Australia's early computer pioneers worked hard to convince investors that a computer was worth building. Write a letter to your teachers, convincing them to let you build your own 2.5-tonne computer in your school.
- Another of Australia's early computers was called UTECOM: University of Technology's Electronic Computer. Around the world there was also WREDAC, EDVAC, ACE, DEUCE, SWAC, SEAC, ABC, UNIVAC, RAMAC, ZEBRA and PEGASUS. What do you think these names stood for?
- SILLIAC was made possible thanks to the generosity of Sir Adolph Basser, a Polish immigrant who never went to university and started his career selling spectacles. What role do you think individuals can play in changing history? Write a story where one person's action transforms the world.

1950 on:
Toilet paper, the Additron and Bertie the Brain

Computer thingies were worth a small fortune and took up most of a room. Back in 1950, you'd be lucky to even see a computer, let alone use one. So computers were special. Precious. Valuable, super-serious machines. Right?

Erm. Sure. Most of the time.

So what was the first computer game? Well, what counts as a computer game depends on your idea of what counts as a computer, and what counts as a game.

But if you count vacuum tubes and light bulbs as a computer ...

... then maybe the first computer game was a 4-metre-tall brain called Bertie.

The tech: Bertie the Brain
Invented by: Josef Kates

Nazis, arrests and prison camp

Josef Kates grew up in children's homes in Germany, didn't enjoy school, and fled from the Nazis when he was a teenager, just before World War II kicked off.

He and his mates escaped to England, but the English thought he was a spy, so he was arrested and sent to a prison camp in Quebec, Canada.

Most of the time, adult inmates at the prison camp were busy cutting wood for 20 cents a day. But in their spare time, some taught school lessons to the prison camp kids. Josef forgot that he didn't like school and decided to soak up all the knowledge he could. He even used toilet paper to make maths and science notebooks.

TP A+

Eventually the prison camp kids were allowed to sit for Canada's official high-school exam. Incredibly, Josef earned the top mark ... and not just the top for the prison camp. For all of Quebec!*

When Josef was finally released, he still wasn't allowed to study at university. Instead, he was given a job making gun sights and periscope prisms. But he still loved maths and physics. At the end of each long day of work, Josef stayed up late studying.

***Josef even beat a fellow kid-prisoner called Walter Kohn. Walter had also escaped from the Nazis, also studied on toilet paper, and went on to win the 1998 Nobel Prize for Chemistry.**

Behold: The Additron

The war ended and Josef was finally able to study at university. There, he met UTEC—the University of Toronto Electronic Computer—one of the world's first electronic computers.

UTEC was huge. And clunky. And, OMG, *annoying*. So Josef set out to improve it. He invented a miniature vacuum tube that could do the job of ten ordinary vacuum tubes. He called it the Additron.

Computer Brain Win!

Josef wanted a way to show ordinary people what the Additron could do.

He came up with Bertie the Brain, a 4-metre tall Additron-powered computer that was expert at tic-tac-toe.

Bertie was probably the world's first electronic opponent. It could work out where to place its next move, based on the moves already made, and it had different difficulty settings, so humans could have at least some chance of winning.

When Bertie went on display in the 1950 Canadian National Exhibition, it was an instant hit.

'It was a much bigger success than we thought. There was always people surrounding it, lining up to play.' Josef Kates

Bertie the Billionaire?

Unfortunately for Josef, around the time Bertie the Brain was Additron-ing its way to celebrity, a team at Bell Labs was having success with an even tinier innovation: the solid-state transistor.

'If the solid-state revolution had started ten years later, I would have been a billionaire.' Josef Kates

Into the future

Josef didn't stop with Bertie the Brain.

He applied what he'd learned with Bertie to create an early computer-controlled traffic signalling system. From tic, tac, toe to green, orange, red.

What would you do?

- **Humans love games, and there are many other contenders for the title of First Ever Computer Game. One so-called 'game' was Bouncing Ball, released in 1951. The game involved watching a pixelated ball bounce around in real-time. Oooh, fun. Bouncing Ball was amazing for demonstrating the laws of physics, but rubbish in terms of being a game, because there was no way to actually play it. So ... not really a game, then. How would you use modern computer technology to change Bouncing Ball into a game that kids would love to play?**
- **After the National Exhibition, Bertie the Brain was forgotten as Josef worked day and night to earn three university qualifications in three subjects in just three years. What do you think should have happened to Bertie? Imagine a different ending for the world's first computer brain.**

PART TWO

GETTING PERSONAL

1944 on: Grandma COBOL, alarm clocks and a giant moth

01001000 01100101 01101100 01101100 01101111 00100001

Unless you speak binary, that sequence probably just looks like a bunch of zeroes and ones. That's what I see, too. Speaking binary is 01110100 01110010 01101001 01100011 01101011 01111001. And I mean totally.

Which is why, early on in computing, people figured out they could code faster if they didn't have to code in binary. Instead, they created programming languages, which turned the zeroes and ones into actual words:

```
Main-Paragraph.
Display "Hello"
Stop Run.
```

These days, if you want to chat with a computer, you can use any number of languages.

Because, thanks to early programmers like Grandma COBOL, anyone can teach an old computer new tricks.

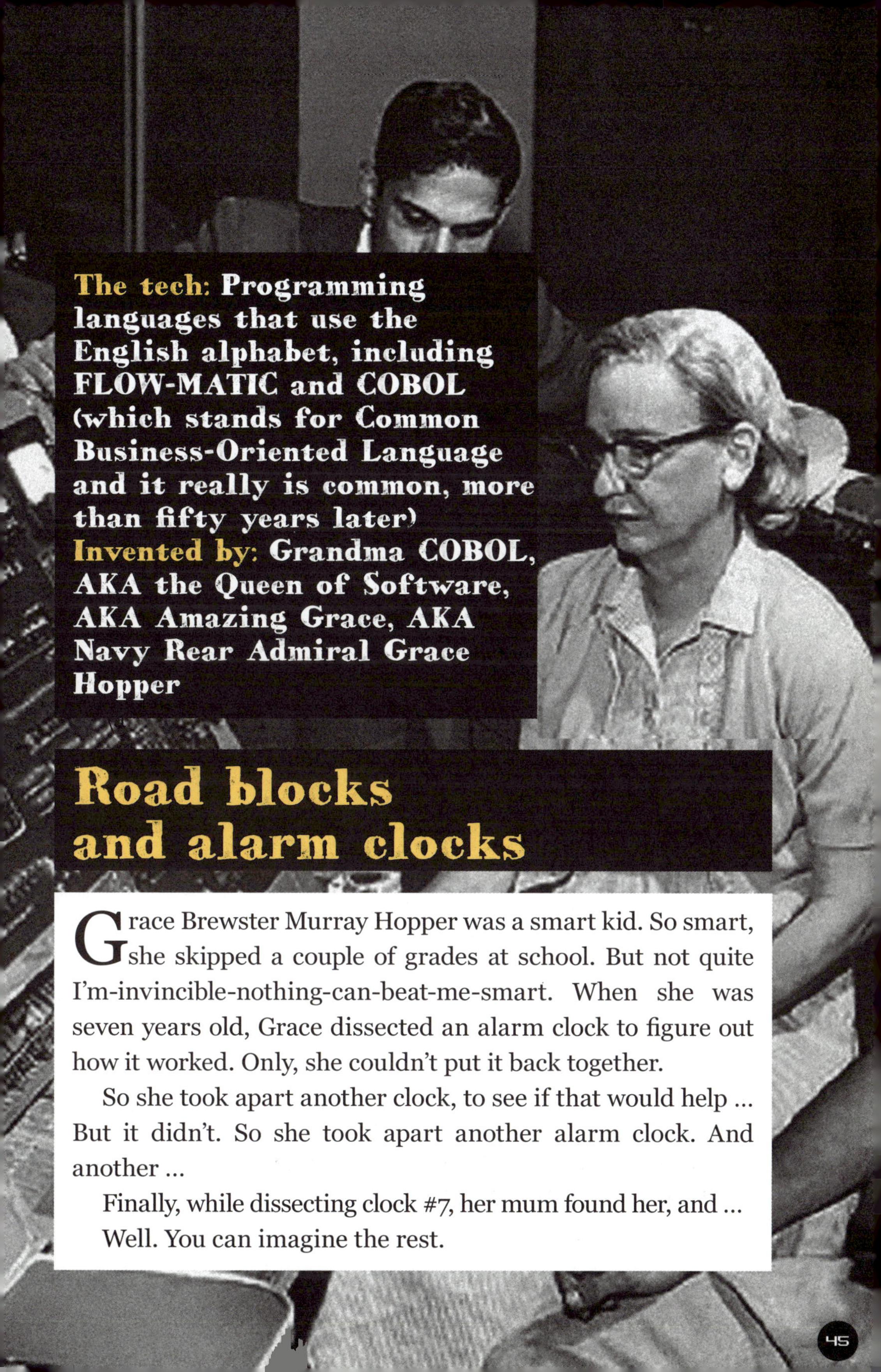

The tech: Programming languages that use the English alphabet, including FLOW-MATIC and COBOL (which stands for Common Business-Oriented Language and it really is common, more than fifty years later)

Invented by: Grandma COBOL, AKA the Queen of Software, AKA Amazing Grace, AKA Navy Rear Admiral Grace Hopper

Road blocks and alarm clocks

Grace Brewster Murray Hopper was a smart kid. So smart, she skipped a couple of grades at school. But not quite I'm-invincible-nothing-can-beat-me-smart. When she was seven years old, Grace dissected an alarm clock to figure out how it worked. Only, she couldn't put it back together.

So she took apart another clock, to see if that would help ... But it didn't. So she took apart another alarm clock. And another ...

Finally, while dissecting clock #7, her mum found her, and ... Well. You can imagine the rest.

Maths + English

Grace was keen to study at uni. Aged sixteen, she failed her first university entrance exam. Not one to give up (see 'alarm clocks', above), she tried again, passed, and made it into uni.

Grace loved university life, and when she finished her studies, she started work as a maths lecturer.

Right from the start, Grace knew communication was vital. She was infamous for making her students write long, wordy essays about maths. Naturally, they complained. A lot. But Grace didn't care. She knew using words to describe numbers was important.

'I would explain, it was no use trying to learn math unless they could communicate it with other people.'
Grace Hopper

Sir, yes, sir!

After the Japanese army bombed Pearl Harbor in World War II, Grace wanted to join the US Navy. So she did. She graduated top of her naval training class and was stoked to be sent to Harvard University, home of the Mark I.

'I was very fortunate ... The navy ordered me to the first big computer in the United States, Mark I at Harvard ... you could put it on a little tiny corner of a chip now.' Grace Hopper

Meet Mark I

Mark I didn't exactly run at the speed of sound (the speed of sound is Mach I, but that's a story for a whole different book). It was, however, an incredible computer for its time.

Mark I:

- weighed 4.5 tonnes (about the same as 10,000 iPad Airs)
- was the size of a large room: more than 15 metres long and 2.4 metres tall
- contained more than 760,000 parts
- used around 800 kilometres of wire to control actual electromechanical switches, which click-clacked back and forth when it was operating
- could complete around three commands every second, so something like multiplying numbers could take six seconds; dividing them took 15+ seconds
- was the first automatic digital calculator in the US

'There was this large mass of machinery. It was all bare, all open, and very noisy.' **Grace Hopper**

From real-world to code

The boss of Mark I was Howard Aiken, a Harvard professor who'd dreamed up the idea when he was just a student. When he was a kid, Howard dropped out of high school to look after his family after his drunk father walked out on them. Young Howard got a job installing telephones to help pay the family's bills, but he studied at night school after work, and slowly worked his way to studying at Harvard.*

Howard was a driven and brilliant guy, but he wasn't always patient.

*Coincidentally, he was also the high-school dropout who climbed into a dusty Harvard University attic in 1937 ... and discovered some of Charles Babbage's Difference Engine.

'Where the hell have you been? Here, compute the coefficients of the arc tangent series by next Thursday.' Howard Aiken to Grace Hopper, when she turned up on her first day (according to Grace)

So Grace learned to program the Mark I, and fast. She shared the work with teammate Richard Bloch. They each worked alternating twelve-hour shifts, so the Mark I was in nonstop 24/7 use.

Grace specialised in talking to engineers and scientists about what they wanted Mark I to do, then nutting out how to get the computer to do it. She became expert at translating technical detail into code.

'I learned languages of oceanography, of this whole business of mine-sweeping, of detonators, of proximity fuses, of biomedical stuff. We had to learn their vocabularies in order to be able to run their problems.' Grace Hopper

Grace would write the code, then program it into the Mark I, which was as easy as punching the right holes into the right places on the right rolls of paper tape, and feeding them into the machine in the right order—which is not actually that easy, but back in the 1940s, this was relatively easy and still super-impressive.

Debugging

Once, when Harvard's Mark II computer stopped, a large moth was found squashed inside the machine.

Despite popular belief, this was not the birth of the terms 'bug' and 'debugging', both of which already existed. The programmers did find it very amusing however and actually taped the dead moth into their logs.

Shortcuts and subroutines

Ada Lovelace predicted it in the 1800s. Grace Hopper perfected it in the 1940s. Both women realised that programming a computer would be easier if you first created a library of mini-codes, like coding shortcuts.

Called 'subroutines', these mini-codes are sections of code you need to use over and over again. Coders still rely on subroutine libraries today.

Version zero

Grace went on to program UNIVAC, the groundbreaking computer developed by inventors Presper Eckert and John Mauchly after their work with ENIAC.

As Grace began to teach computers more and more complicated things, her programs grew more and more complicated, too. Which was obviously a pain. What Grace needed was a program to help her write programs.

So she wrote one. Today, we call this type of program a compiler.

Grace's compiler was the first, and she called it A-0, for Arithmetic Language Version Zero.

How pragmatic

Grace kept working on A-0, then she developed A-1, A-2, A-3 (called ARITH-MATIC), AT-3 (called MATH-MATIC) and B-0 (called FLOW-MATIC).

She was always looking to improve her code, so she'd send it to friends and colleagues for their contributions and advice. This same process—sharing code instead of keeping it secret—is still used today by the Open Source software community.

COBOL

In 1959, Grace co-developed the COBOL programming language.

More than fifty years later, computers all around the globe are still using COBOL. Programmers have written hundreds of billions of lines in COBOL code.

```
IDENTIFICATION DIVISION.
PROGRAM-ID. ACobolHello.
* how to say hello
PROCEDURE DIVISION.
    DISPLAY 'Hello!'.
    STOP RUN.
```

Into the future

Grace served the US Navy for forty-three years. Twice, she tried to retire early, but each time, the US Congress changed the rules so she could be called back to active duty. When she finally actually retired from the Navy, she was seventy-nine years old.

Even then, Grace didn't stop. She took a job with DEC, now called Hewlett-Packard, and set out to inspire new programmers.

'They come to me, you know, and say, "Do you think we can do this?" I say, "Try it."' Grace Hopper

What would you do?

- **Grace Hopper's boss, Howard Aiken, asked her to write down everything she knew about how to program the Mark I. She ended up with a 500-page book. Can you think of anything so interesting and complicated that you could write 500 pages about it? What would you love to read 500 pages about?**
- **The COBOL programming language is still common, even fifty years after its invention. What other inventions have survived that long?**

1947 on: Germanium, jealousy and the transistor

There are more than two billion transistors in a smartphone. To keep up with demand, factories are producing around 8 trillion transistors per second per day. That's more transistors in a second than there are stars in the Milky Way or galaxies in the universe.

One estimate suggests we've made more than 2,900,000,000,000,000,000,000 transistors.

The tech: **The transistor: an on–off switch that can boost an electric current**
Invented by: **John Bardeen, Walter Brattain and William Shockley, all from Bell Labs**

~~Switches~~ ~~Vacuum tubes~~ Something!?

The first computer switches were actual real-life switches: levers that flicked up and down, or swung left and right. All this flicking and swinging meant early computers were stuck in go-slow mode. How slow? Test it for yourself: Try flicking a light switch on and off as fast as you can. How fast can *you* go? Try as hard as you like, you're never going to get even a teensy bit close to the speed of a modern computer switch.

Vacuum tubes were a huge step up from mechanical switches. They could switch on and off as fast as an electric current could be generated in a wire (around the speed of light, if you were wondering). And thanks to vacuum tubes we had radio, TV, telephone and radar, so I don't want to be too hard on them. But honestly? They sucked. They took up loads of space, overheated all the time and broke almost as often.

The computing world was ready for something way, way better. But what?

The Idea Factory

Does the name Alexander Graham Bell ring a _ _ _ _?

That's right, he's the telephone guy. Well, with some of the dosh he made from selling telephones, Alexander started a research laboratory. He not-so-modestly named it Bell Labs, AKA, 'The Idea Factory'.

Alexander's plan was to plonk thousands of clever people into one building and then let them invent stuff. It worked.

The cow-herd and the theorist

William Shockley's job at Bell Labs was to invent a replacement for vacuum tubes. He needed to create a smaller, more efficient on–off switch that could also amplify electric signals. It was a crazy-big ask, so he recruited a team of experts to get the job done.

Two of his team, Walter Brattain and John Bardeen, shared an office.

'It was probably one of the greatest research teams ever pulled together.' Walter Brattain

Walter grew up on a ranch, herding cows. He was clever at making stuff.

John was so smart he skipped three years of school. He was terrific at theory.

Together, Walter and John tried and failed and tried and failed again to find a way to amplify an electronic signal.

Then eventually, on 16 December 1947, something ~~tiny~~ huge happened. The pair created the transistor.

Their design used two super-slim bits of gold and a mini chunk of germanium. When they ran a small electric current through the gold, they noticed that a much larger current ran through the germanium. Amplification!

And when they stopped the current in the gold, it stopped in the germanium. An on–off switch!

The transistor wasn't pretty, and it only worked when they wriggled its parts around, but it did the job. They'd invented a replacement for the vacuum tube.

What's in a name?

Time for a quick vote: what's the catchiest name for this new invention?

a) Semi-conductor triode
b) Surface-state amplifier
c) Transistor

The Bell Labs team took a vote, and—thank goodness—'transistor' was the winner.

The name was suggested by an engineer (and science-fiction author) called JJ Coupling (real name: John Pierce).

'After growing wildly for years, the field of computing appears to be reaching its infancy.'
John Pierce

German geraniums

The first transistors were made from germanium, a rare, silvery element discovered in Germany and not named after geraniums. Today's transistors are made from silicon, so they're basically bits of high-tech sand.

Opposites attract

Electricity is just teensy-weensy particles called electrons moving around. Electrons have a negative charge, so they go racing after anything that has a positive charge. This creates an electric current.

By controlling charge, you can control where electrons go. If you can control where electrons go, you can create a transistor. And if you link a bunch of transistors together, you create an integrated circuit, or microchip. And then something the size of a matchbox can replace something the size of a semi-trailer filled with matchboxes. And it's quieter, too.

Three's a crowd

Walter and John quickly shared the news of their invention, but William was jealous. First, he demanded credit for their idea, then he secretly decided to go one better. Working like a lonely spy in the night, William built on their invention, creating the sandwich-style transistor we still use today.

How to make a sandwich-style transistor:

1. Take a piece of silicon and trap some extra electrons in it, giving it a negative charge. This is called an n-type semiconductor.
2. Take a different piece of silicon and steal some electrons from it, giving it a positive charge. This is called a p-type semiconductor.

This is a replica of the first transistor Walter, John and William made. Today, billions of transistors can be crammed onto a CPU a few centimetres across. The XBox One CPU for example has 5 billion transistors. Photo: Windell Oskay

3. Cram a layer of p-type between two layers of n-type. This is called a sandwich.
4. Now run a positive voltage through the middle p-type layer. This will suck in negative electrons, causing a current. The bigger the voltage, the more the electrons move.

In 1956, all three inventors shared the Nobel Prize for Physics. But that didn't help their friendship. Walter and John felt betrayed by William's secrecy. The team broke up, and Walter and John were never again BFFs with William.

Into the future

After things turned sour with Walter and John, William left to form his own company. He not-so-modestly called it Shockley Semiconductor Laboratory, and he set up in the Santa Clara Valley, California.*

But it sucks to be William. He was such a grumpy boss that eight of his best employees left him. Called the 'traitorous eight', they started their own company: Fairchild Semiconductor.

Two of the 'traitorous eight' eventually started another company: Intel Corporation. Their names were Bob Noyce and Gordon Moore.

Gordon famously predicted that the number of transistors able to fit on a microchip would double every year. This prediction—known as Moore's Law—held for more than fifty years.

***You may have heard of the spot? Today it's known as Silicon Valley.**

What would you do?

- **Bell Labs patented the transistor, to protect their invention. Then they licensed it at a super-cheap rate, so other companies could make and use it. Why do you think they were so quick to share their invention? What would you have done?**
- **What do you think makes a successful team? What can you do to ensure your team works well together?**

1960s on: Moon landings, LOL memory and (it really is) rocket science

When you're strapped into a glorified tin can being rocketed from Earth at a zillion miles an hour, you kinda-sorta want the world's best technology on your side.

Only, back in the 1960s, the world's best technology was somewhere between a fridge and a pocket calculator.

Still, you can trust your toaster to get you safely into orbit ... right?

The tech: Calculations and computing required to send humans to the moon
Worked out by: Human computers and coders including Katherine Johnson, Annie Easley, Margaret Hamilton and more

Crash course

In case you've forgotten, the moon is a giant hunk of non-cheese that regularly appears in our night sky. Though it sometimes seems quite close, it's actually more than 356,000 kilometres away.

And how far is 356,000 kilometres? Well, jump in a car of your choosing, then drive from the far west of Australia all the way to the far east, then turn around and drive back again. Now repeat that forty-four times. It's about that far.

Give or take a kilometre

The moon is hurtling through space. And so are we. So, if you want to land on the moon without becoming a burning hunk of space junk, 'around 356,000 kilometres' away isn't going to cut it. You want to be totally exact. Because no-one wants to blast off on a moon voyage without being 100 per cent abso-positively convinced that the numbers are accurate.

'If you have a basketball and a baseball 14 feet [about 4 metres] apart, where the baseball represents the moon and the basketball represents the Earth, and you take a piece of paper sideways, the thinness of the paper would be the corridor you have to hit when you come back.' Astronaut David Scott, on returning from the moon

So who you gonna call? Computers.

Wind-tunnel maths

Before computer simulations, there were a couple of sweet ways to work out if your newly invented machine could fly:

1. **Fly it.** Pros: Quite fun (for a short while) Cons: Possibly quite deadly (permanently). Also, expensive.
2. **Put it in a wind tunnel.** Pros: Less expensive, less deadly. Cons: OMG, so much maths!!!

Wind tunnels aren't actual tunnels, they're more like try-hard sheds. Back in the '60s, they contained huge fans that created wind. By measuring how wind moved around the test aeroplane, engineers could work out how to improve the shape of their flying machines.

Unfortunately, this involved a whole wind-tunnel-load of complicated maths.

Luckily, there were computers for that: *human* computers.

From Mercury to Apollo

Human computers did heaps of maths to design the rockets and direct the flight path of several space missions, including:

- the Project Mercury missions (when we were still figuring out how to orbit Earth)
- Apollo 11 (when Neil Armstrong and his pals flew to the moon)
- Apollo 13 (when the mission didn't make it to the moon because an on-board oxygen tank exploded and the

crew had to do some crazy-clever makeshift repairs before they could attempt to return safely to Earth … Did they make it??? You'll never find out! Never!*)

*Spoiler alert: Yes, they did. You should totally see the movie.

Mercury-Atlas 6 mission

Katherine Johnson was a NASA Space Task Force technologist, but she started out as a human computer. She did some mind-bending maths for the Mercury-Atlas 6 mission.

MA-6 was the United States' first-ever attempt to send an astronaut into orbit. The astronaut's name was John Glenn, and he was pretty mega-brave. Back then, there was no way of knowing what blasting into space could do to a human, and there was certainly no guarantee that John would come back.

As well as being mega-brave, John was careful. Even though the box-computers had calculated his flight path, John asked John asked human computer Katherine to calculate everything again to calculate everything again. Just to be sure.

Up for the challenge

Katherine did all the maths herself, taking hours and hours of super-stressful work. One itty-bitty mistake and it would be bye-bye John.

But Katherine's calculations were spot on: her answers matched the computer's answers. John was satisfied, and took to the skies.

John's mission was a success, paving the way for future

missions to the moon. His mission also provided some pretty compelling proof that all those electrons and wires could be trusted to produce the right results, paving the way for a computing revolution.

The NASA life

Even as a tiny kid, Katherine loved maths, counting everything from footsteps to forks. Katherine started high school when she was just ten years old. When she was eighteen, she finished uni, getting top marks in maths and French. She started working as a maths teacher, which she loved.

But Katherine wanted something more ... When she was thirty-four, she heard about some sweet maths jobs going at the National Advisory Committee for Aeronautics (NACA, soon to become NASA—the 'S' stands for 'space'). Katherine applied for a job ... and missed out.

The next year, she tried again ... and got the job!

Katherine went on to work for NASA for thirty-three years, right up to 1986.

'I was doing something I liked doing every day, came to work happy to be here and enjoyed doing it all the time.' Katherine Johnson

When I grow up, I want to be ...

Annie Easley had always wanted to be a nurse. Unfortunately, her local uni didn't offer the right course, so Annie didn't know what to do.

Um. Um. Um.

Then she heard about NACA's maths jobs and realised she'd always wanted to be a mathematician.

'It doesn't matter what your age is or what you decide to do when you're eighteen or sixteen, it doesn't matter if you change your mind later on and change fields, because we need to be flexible.'
Annie Easley

Annie got the job. She worked at NASA for thirty-four years. She started as a human computer, and when computers became machines, she became a programmer, working on software for rockets, hybrid vehicles and beyond.

'You can be anything you want to. It doesn't matter what you look like, what your size is, what your colour is. You can be anything you want to, but you do have to work at it.' Annie Easley, quoting her mother's advice

The Apollo Guidance Commputer, or AGC, and its control interface DSKY (DiSplay and KeYboard) ...

Apollo Guidance Computer

The Apollo Guidance Computer was a no-crash hot piece of technology. It was in charge of getting rockets safely to the moon. Compared to today's tech, its brain was the approximate speed and size of a reluctant pea.

But for its time, the AGC was incredible. It was ...

- **probably the world's first embedded computer:** an entire computer, wired up to work inside another computer—the 13,000-kilogram spacecraft.
- **super-light:** it used transistors to form around 4000 integrated circuits (the grandparents of today's microchips). At one stage, NASA had ordered and used more than half of the world's integrated circuits!
- **user-friendly:** astronauts could operate it literally with the push of a button. And if the astronauts freaked out and forgot which button because of hurtling at top-speed through the cold, dark vacuum of space, there was a printout of instructions stuck to the wall. Phew.

Coding cardboard

Like Ada Lovelace, Margaret Hamilton's dad was a poet. And like Ada, Margaret fell in love with the logic of maths. She became a gun programmer and led a team of hundreds of coders to create the software for the Apollo missions.

Want to try coding Apollo software? Here's what you have to do:

- Work out what you want the computer to do, then use a language called MAC (MIT Algebraic Compiler) to code its instructions.
- Translate your MAC code into zeroes and ones, so the computer can understand.
- Turn those zeroes and ones into a coded pattern of holes.
- Punch those holes into bits of cardboard and feed the cardboard into a computer that can simulate the moon landing while you're still on Earth.
- Test your code, and retest and cross-test and double-check-test until you're happy.
- Then (and this is the killer), **weave** your code into mini magnetic rings using long copper wires: if you thread a

Margaret Hamilton at NASA in 1969. That huge stack of paper next to her? That's the code she and her team wrote for Apollo, which was then woven into the memory of the AGC.

wire *through* a ring, that's a 1; if you thread the wire *outside* the ring, that's a 0.*

And now fly to the moon. Too easy.

'We used to go to the cafeteria and the astronauts would come in [and] thank us for what a good job we were doing.' Mary Lou Rogers, who helped weave Apollo's read-only memory into its wires

***The weaving team was nicknamed the Little Old Ladies, so the woven code was called 'LOL memory' for short.**

Error! Error!

The AGC was fab, but you couldn't ask it to do two things at once. If you did, you'd overload the computer, and up would flash the dreaded '1202' error code. Which could be kind of tricky if you were, say, flying to the moon.

In an epic example of awful timing, the 1202 error popped up when Neil Armstrong and Buzz Aldrin were inside the *Eagle* lunar module, dropping to the surface of the moon for the first time in history ...

`1202.`

`1202.`

Not one to panic (PANIC!!!??!!), Neil asked Mission Control what to do.

Mission Control wasn't sure, so they asked other people in the room what to do.

Most people didn't have a clue, but coder Jack Garman knew the answer. He said, 'Don't worry about it right now, because you're landing on the moon, dudes.' Or something like that.

As a member of the coding team, Jack knew the software inside-out, and he was confident things would be okay. So the computer was spitting its dummy because it could only do one thing at a time. No problem, because it was programmed to do the most important thing first. And the most important thing was landing safely.

Neil and Buzz ignored the error and the *Eagle* landed A-OK. That's one small step for man, one giant leap for the IT Help Desk.

Into the future

NASA is now preparing for a human journey to Mars, hoping to land astronauts on an asteroid by 2025, and on Mars during the 2030s. To achieve this, they'll need the very best scientists, engineers and computer coders. How old will you be in 2025? Maybe the perfect age to apply ...

What would you do?

- **Back when Katherine and Annie were working at NASA, women were paid less than men for doing the same job, and this was considered normal. Also, black people were given fewer opportunities than white people, and this was considered normal, too. Do you think these differences still exist today? What do you think about these issues?**
- **Imagine you're applying for the job of astronaut to go to Mars. Write a resume listing your skills and explaining why they're important. Can you convince the selection panel to choose you?**

1968 on: The Memex, the Mother of All Demos and the Microbee

So hang on a sec. We now have microchips. We now have programming languages. But computers are still the size of a room and the price of a house? And they're still controlled by someone else?

Um. I don't think that's going to cut it. In fact, I think the whole computer scene is about to get personal.

The tech: An entire computer memory and all just for you
Controlled by: You. That's right. A personal computer. Just for you (alright, and your family). It even sits on your desk.

Meet your memex

Back in 1945, a guy called Vannevar (rhymes with 'beaver') Bush had an idea:

'Consider a future device for individual use, which is a sort of mechanized private file and library ... It is an enlarged intimate supplement to his memory.' Vannevar Bush

Vannevar named this device the 'memex', but he could have called it the PC. Or the iPad. And Vannevar wasn't the only one dreaming of a personal computer.

The Mother of All Demos

When Douglas Engelbart read about Vannevar's memex, his brain exploded*.

'The whole concept of helping people work and think that way just excited me.' Douglas Engelbart

Doug got stuck into figuring out ways to make machines and people work together. Then, in 1968, he showed his ideas to nearly 1000 people. His presentation became known as the Mother of All Demos. It took just ninety minutes, but it impressed the pants off everyone**, and pretty much changed the world.

He demonstrated many state-of-the-art, mind-blowing technologies:

Behold! The cursor!

Presenting ... the mouse!

Check it right out! Each program appears in its own window!

And he showed that he could link his computer with a friend's computer at a nearby uni.

***This is a metaphor.**
****This is probably a metaphor.**

Alan Kay digs it

Alan Kay was sick as a dog on the day he flew to see Doug's Mother of All Demos.

'I was shivering and sick and could barely walk, but I was determined to get there.' **Alan Kay**

But it was totally worth it. Alan loved what he saw.

Years later, when Alan took a job with Xerox PARC (Palo Alto Research Centre), he worked to bring many of Doug's ideas to reality:

- **Bitmapping:** A way to turn every single pixel on your computer's monitor on or off independently, so you can draw cool pictures, use cool fonts and play cool games
- **Ethernet:** A way to link computers in an office, like making a mini-internet
- **Computer mouse:** Every time you click, thank Doug.

Invent the future

Alan's Aussie dad was a biologist and Alan's mum was a musician. The family lived in Australia for a few years when Alan was a kid.

'By the time I got to school, I had already read a couple of hundred books ... One book I read was called *Rockets, Missiles, and Space Travel* by Willi Ley. The thing that struck me was that when you go from one planet to another, you wouldn't go the way you thought you would. You don't aim the rocket ship at the planet, you aim the rocket ship at where the planet is going to be.' Alan Kay

This became the basis of Alan's entire philosophy, and of what was perhaps his most famous quote:

'The best way to predict the future is to invent it.' Alan Kay

Smalltalk, big vision

Alan's dream was to create a personal computer simple enough that kids could use it (and cheap enough that their parents could afford it!). He called it the Dynabook. He created a programming language for kids to use too, called Smalltalk. And he worked hard on his dream. (Pretty. Much. All. The. Time.)

‘A lot of daytime was spent outside of PARC, playing tennis, bike riding, drinking beer, eating Chinese food, and constantly talking about the Dynabook.’ Alan Kay

Me like ~~cookies~~ bitmapping

Although Alan’s Dynabook was never made, an ‘interim Dynabook’ got the go-ahead. Alan and the PARC team called it the Xerox Alto. To show off its bitmapping ability, the team included a picture of Cookie Monster with the letter ‘C’.

Xerox made a couple of thousand Altos, but the Xerox bosses were all like, ‘Yay, photocopiers’ and didn’t really understand the potential.

‘The computer will never be as important to society as the copier.’ unnamed Xerox Boss

Me like Xerox Alto too ...

Lucky for us, someone else saw what the PARC team had created.

That someone was a guy named Steve Jobs*. In 1979, Steve J took a quick tour of Xerox PARC to clock what Alan had on offer ...

Steve’s eyes totally bugged out. After the tour, he hotfooted it home and started work.

He wasn’t the first to see the Alto.

***You may have heard of Steve? He co-founded a little company called Apple ...**

'Many people (perhaps even a thousand or more) had seen live demos of the Alto and Smalltalk before Steve.' Alan Kay

But he was the first to grab onto the Alto's potential with both hands and start sprinting down the street, whooping with excitement*.

***Not sure if this is a metaphor.**

Microbee takes off

Meanwhile, in Australia ...

Owen Hill and a just-out-of-high-school kid called Matthew Starr were working on their own PC. Owen and Matt called it the Microbee, and by 1982 they were selling it.

While IBM, Apple and Commodore owned the northern hemisphere, Microbee sold like hot cakes in the south (and sold well in Sweden and Russia too).

Into the future

Tens of thousands of Microbees were shipped. Schools across Australia used them in classrooms, new models were created and released, and for a while it looked like Microbee might fly forever. Sadly, however, it just couldn't compete with the bigger companies.

What would you do?

- Microbee started out with the not-so-cool codename Edcom. But Owen and Matt wanted something friendly and easy to remember, so they changed it to Microbee. How important do you think a name is to a product's popularity? Think of some popular products with dud names. What would you rename them?
- After Microbee went broke, Owen took his skills and ideas and launched a new company, called Earthsafe. Think of a time when something you did didn't work out. Were you able to take those skills and ideas and apply them to something new?
- Alan Kay famously said the best way to predict the future is to invent it. Draw and label a device that could be useful in the future. What does it do? How is it helpful? Does it help us live more sustainably?

Before we move on, check out the very first computer mouse, as designed by Doug. You can see one of the two wheels on the underside that it used to move a cursor on a display.

1970s on: The Tuesday club, flipped pancakes and speeding fines

Software used to be hardware's sad second-cousin: no-one thought it was particularly talented or good-looking. In fact, it came free and pre-installed with your computer. Because seriously, who cares about software, right?

Then one day in December 1974, a maths student named Bill Gates started to wonder: what if you made it so software was the more-significant other? What if the codes that controlled your computer became more important than the computer?

The tech: Microsoft BASIC
Invented by: Bill Gates, Paul Allen and a bunch of pizza-eating, Coke-drinking, code-writing kids

Focused on success

All his life, Bill Gates wanted to win. As a kid, he spent hours perfecting particular skills—like serving a tennis ball, memorising a speech, or jumping out of a rubbish bin. (Seriously.)

'Be careful—it can hurt if you don't succeed.'
Bill Gates, on jumping over office chairs and out of rubbish bins

Despite his fixation with jumping, Bill was super-smart. But he didn't always get on with non-genius kids.

Bill's list of awesome insults

- That's stupid
- That's the stupidest thing I've ever heard
- That's completely brain dead

All about Bill:

- His real name is William Henry Gates III.
- His childhood nickname was Trey, from the French word for 'three'.
- He was mega-ambitious, hoping one day to own a software company employing thirty-five programmers!!!

High-school hacker

At high school, Bill taught himself how to code. Before school, after school, at lunchtime, even late into the night.

Bill and his mates would crowd around the school's only computer terminal. The terminal connected to an off-site time-shared computer, owned by a computer company. Connecting to the computer cost $4.80/minute, paid for by the school's parents' association. (Thanks, mums and dads!)

But, Bill figured, why pay to play?

He and pal Paul Allen hacked their way into free accounts. Whee! Then they were both caught and banned from using the computer for months. Not-whee!

'I swore off computers for a while, and I tried to be normal ... Instead I read biographies of Napoleon and novels like *Catcher in the Rye*.' Bill Gates

Learning from mistakes ...

A year later, when computing time was $15/hour, sixteen-year-old Bill and his mates hacked in again. Again, they were caught.

To avoid being re-banned, they offered to write free software for the computer company. Oh, and they said they'd work in exchange for free computer time. Their offer was accepted.

The kids used COBOL (remember Grace Hopper?) to write software for the company's payroll. In exchange, they received $18,000 worth of free computer time.

Computer crashers club

Meanwhile, Bill and his school friends had named their computer club. They called it the Lakeside Programming Group.

With such a serious name, they started to attract serious attention. Computer companies offered them free samples, and even programming contracts! Soon the club was recruited to test-drive a new computer*. Awesome! Even awesomer, there was a pizza place right across the road.

*They worked with Steve Russell, nickname 'Slug', the creator of one of the very first computer games, *Spacewar*.

Mission: Test-drive

Attention: Fellow members of the Lakeside Programming Group

Our mission: Crash this new computer as many times as possible, to discover all its hidden faults. Preferred technique: Spend day and night reading and memorising computer manuals, then code and game like crazy to push the machine to its absolute limits. Also, pizza.

'Trey got so into it that he would sneak out the basement door after we went to bed and spend most of the night there.' Bill Gates' dad

Dumpster diving

Bill and his mates knew they could learn faster if they could get their hands on the machine's source code (the instructions for how to program the computer). But source code was off-limits for mere schoolkids, until ...

One night, Paul helped Bill climb into a skip bin out the back of the building. Bill searched through all the rubbish till he found printouts of the source code.

'We took that precious hoard back to the terminal room and pored over it for hours.' Paul Allen

Tuesday Club

While still at school, Bill was put in charge of writing software to schedule his entire school's classes. He delivered a piece of software that avoided all clashes, managed all the classrooms, and gave Bill and his mates Tuesday afternoons off. They called themselves the Tuesday Club and had matching T-shirts printed.

Bill's list of fun stuff for the weekend

Bill was super-intelligent, super-focused, and loved super-extreme living. Fun stuff to do:

- **Buy a red Mustang convertible and zoom around at top speed**
- **Go kite-skiing behind a mad-fast speedboat**
- **Make a million dollars before I turn thirty***

***Whoops. He actually made $350 million before age thirty.**

Bill's list of rebellious stuff for the weekend

Bill also hated rules, sometimes for no reason. Crazy stuff to do:

- **Don't attend any of the classes I'm enrolled in: only attend classes I'm not enrolled in**
- **Don't write software before I try to sell it: sell it first, then write it later**
- **Don't leave pancake piles untidy: break world record for untidy pancake stacks**

Bill's record-breaking maths assignment

Here is the pancake-sorting maths question that Bill aced at Harvard University:

The chef in our place is sloppy, and when he prepares a stack of pancakes they come out all different sizes. Therefore, when I deliver them to a customer, on the way to the table I rearrange them (so that the smallest winds up on top, and so on, down to the largest at the bottom) by grabbing several from the top and flipping them over, repeating this (varying the number I flip) as many times as necessary. If there are n pancakes, what is the maximum number of flips (as a function of n) that I will ever have to use to rearrange them?

Bill's answer: Around 1.67 flips per pancake.

Micro-Soft is born

When Bill was still at university*, he and Paul wrote the software that would make them famous. They designed it so computer fans could write their own BASIC programs on the new Altair 8800 microcomputer.

The challenge was to fit their entire piece of software into just 4000 bytes: the only memory available.

Bill and Paul competed to see who could code a particular task using the fewest lines. They finally completed the entire program using just 3200 bytes (around one page of text).

They called their creation Micro-Soft BASIC, which soon became good-old Microsoft.

***How cool are universities? Way cool. You can meet new people, learn new things, share knowledge, and experiment with strange haircuts.**

The Altair 8800 didn't actually come with a cool clear case back in 1975.

Weekly schedule:

- Code nonstop for days
- Pass out for around eighteen hours
- Wake up, stretch, start coding again
- Insert pizza as required

Pirate treasure

In 1975, a copy of the punch tape encoding Microsoft BASIC ended up with the Homebrew Computer Club*.

The club believed software should be free, so member Dan Sokol sneakily made copies of the tape for his pals. Soon people everywhere were happily using and distributing the pirated software.

Twenty-year-old Bill was outraged**. He'd worked day and night to code the software, and now it was being given away for free. Where was the respect!?

Bill calculated that 90 per cent of BASIC's users hadn't paid for the software. This meant he was earning just $2/hour for all that time he'd spent coding.

But there was unexpected treasure in all those pirate copies: Microsoft BASIC was suddenly everywhere. So many people were using BASIC that it quickly became the standard in software. By the time Microsoft followed up with Microsoft Windows years later, people didn't think twice about which software they wanted to buy.

*Among the club's computaholic members were two soon-to-be-Apple-famous Steves: Steve Jobs and Steve Wozniak.
**Bill perhaps forgot that he'd also hacked his way into free computer stuff once or twice. The Microsoft code, for example, was mostly written using a free account on his university computer.

QDOS for MS-DOS

Then Microsoft, almost accidentally, scored a tidy contract to make software for hardware giant IBM. (Another company was lined up to do it, but the boss went flying in his private plane on the day of the IBM meeting, so Bill got the job instead.)

Unfortunately, Microsoft didn't actually have time to build the software they'd promised. So instead, they bought some sort-of-okay software from another company, then worked to make it better.

The team turned QDOS, or the Quick and Dirty Operating System, into MS-DOS, the Microsoft Disc Operating System.

IBM loved MS-DOS, only they changed the name to PC-DOS: Personal Computer Disc Operating System.

DOS became the standard operating system for decades.

```
C:/DOS
C:/DOS/RUN
RUN/DOS/RUN
```

Into the future

Microsoft went on to become the world's largest software company, offering software for email, internet, gaming and more. Worth around US$200 billion, Microsoft employs more than 100,000 people. Slightly more than the thirty-five Bill was aiming for.

What would you do?

- In the early days of Microsoft, Bill celebrated by buying a Porsche 911 and speeding around. He was caught and ended up in jail. Once he received three speeding tickets in a single trip. Do you think recklessness is important in innovation? Do you think Bill's behaviour was appropriate?
- Software was once the giveaway that came free when you bought your computer. Products like Microsoft changed this, making software the common element that could run on almost any hardware. Can you think of any other examples where changing our thinking could disrupt the way a market or product works?
- At his peak, Bill was worth over US$100 billion. He and his wife have promised to donate 95 per cent of their money to charities. What would you do in the same situation? Draw up a plan for how you would distribute your cash.

His haircut isn't THAT bad ...

1970s on: Cream soda, blue boxes and the Homebrew Computer Club

Today, Apple rakes in more than US$40 billion in profits each year. And it all started with two kids named Steve.

The tech: Apple I home computer
Invented by: Steve Jobs and Steve Wozniak

Cool stuff I made, by Steve Wozniak

- Grade 2: **Crystal radio**
- Grade 5: **Intercom system for neighbourhood kids to chat**
- Grade 6: **Hallicrafters shortwave radio**
- High school: **Ticking metronome that looks a lot like a bomb. (Update: Principal heard it ticking in my locker and called the bomb squad!!!)**

Hello? It's Kissinger

One day in 1971, Steve W met Steve J, a tech-loving practical joker just five years younger than himself. The two Steves hit it off.

They went to university together and launched one of their first business ideas from their dorm room: making and selling blue boxes.

Blue boxes were hacking technology that let people make free phone calls. The boxes could whistle a whole variety of coded tones, which confused and controlled the telephone exchange. Using a blue box, you could dial almost any phone line you wanted, use it for free, and your home line would stay invisible.

Steve W designed the device. Steve J did the smooth talking, selling them up and down the corridors of their university.

'I've never designed a circuit I was prouder of. I still think it was incredible.' Steve Wozniak

Steve W even used a blue box to prank-call the Pope by pretending to be US politician Henry Kissinger.

Pizza parlour heist

The Steves tried to expand their business when two guys in a pizza shop said they were interested in buying a blue box. Steve J showed them the product, the dudes pulled a gun, stole the box and took off. But strangely, before they escaped, the thieves gave the Steves their phone number.

'They didn't know how to use [the blue box]. They gave us a phone number to call so we could tell them.' Steve Wozniak

Blue box accounting

- Cost to build: $40 worth of parts per box
- Cost to buy: $150 each
- Profit: $110 per box sold! Woot woot!!

Phreaking out

Phone phreakers were hackers who focused on hacking phone lines.

Early phone lines were controlled using a series of specially coded tones. And early phone calls, especially long-distance calls, were expensive. Phreakers specialised in making them free.

The Steves' Blue Boxes were inspired by John Draper, one of the world's first phreakers. Using a whistle he found in a box of Cap'n Crunch cereal, John could instruct the phone system to open a long-distance line, for free!

Get off the phone!

Phreakers became even more powerful after the internet kicked in. This is because all internet connections were made using phone lines. (This was also mega-annoying: most homes had just one phone line, so you couldn't phone a friend and be on the internet at the same time.)

By controlling phone lines, phreakers could connect, disconnect, route and reroute internet connections. This meant they could hack into the world's computers for free, and all from the comfort of their bedroom.

Get a real job

Both Steves started out working for computer companies.

Steve W got a job at Hewlett-Packard, designing electronic calculators.

Steve J worked at Atari, designing computer games. But because he didn't like to shower, or wear shoes, or be polite, his boss gave him the night shift. He also gave him some cunning advice.

'I told him, pretend to be completely in control, and people will assume you are.' Nolan Bushnell, Steve J's boss

Cream Soda power

After work, Steve W spent his time making computers and games. Back then, computers didn't have screens, so he played the games by connecting the computer to his TV.

His favourite trick was to redesign HP computers using fewer computer chips. He designed his own computer to use just twenty chips. It had no screen, no keyboard, and a whole lot of flashing lights.

He built this beast with a friend, and they named it the Cream Soda Computer. This is because when they built it, they were powered by Cragmont cream soda, a sugary, vanilla-flavoured soft drink.

The Homebrew Computer Club

Making computers all alone in your bedroom could be lonely work. That's why this flyer caught Steve W's eye:

Steve ——— 2/17/75

AMATEUR COMPUTER USERS GROUP
HOMEBREW COMPUTER CLUB . . . you name it.

Are you building your own computer? Terminal? T V Typewriter? I/O device? or some other digital black-magic box?

Or are you buying time on a time-sharing service?

If so, you might like to come to a gathering of people with like-minded interests. Exchange information, swap ideas, talk shop, help work on a project, whatever . . .

We are getting together Wednesday nite, March 5th, 7 pm at the home of Gordon French 614 18th Ave., Menlo Park (near Marsh Road).

If you can't make it this time, drop us a card for the next meeting.

See ya there, Fred Moore

Hope you can come.
There will be other Altair builders there.

Steve W was notoriously shy, but he plucked up his courage and went along. It was at this first meeting of the Homebrew Computer Club that he heard about Intel's new microprocessor, a tiny chip with the power to change the world.

'That night turned out to be one of the most important nights of my life ... This whole vision of a personal computer just popped into my head. I started to sketch out on paper what would later become known as the Apple I.' Steve Wozniak

Free, pay here

The Homebrew Computer Club was all about free sharing of their computer love, and Steve W was too. He made dozens of copies of his computer designs and shared them around.

But when Steve J heard about Steve W's work, he had different ideas, and they all came with dollar signs.

'Every time I'd design something great, Steve would find a way to make money for us.' Steve Wozniak

A is for attractive

On April Fool's Day, 1976, on the back of Steve W's awesome designs, the Steves started their own computer company. They named it Apple, because starting with an A was useful for advertising, and perhaps because Steve J sometimes visited an apple orchard.

Steve J wanted Apple computers to be The Very Best. When

they launched the Apple I, they sold all 200 hand-built units. But the Apple I was basically a circuit board: it wasn't very pretty.

By the time Apple II came along in 1977, you could see Steve J's philosophy at work.

Apple IIs were different from other personal computers:

- **they looked amazing:** Steve designed them to look like expensive kitchen appliances
- **they came with preinstalled Apple software:** no option for rubbishy operating systems
- **they weren't designed to be opened:** no amateurs messing with the guts of this gorgeous box.

They sold like hot cakes. Each Apple II cost $1298, more than $6500 in today's money. The Steves moved 100,000 units in just three years.

Apples and apples (Apple I and Apple II)

Great gooey!

GUI (pronounced gooey), stands for Graphical User Interface. GUIs use cool icons and pictures to represent different apps and functions. Like  for storing your files, and  for deleting them.

So who invented GUIs?

Not the Steves, who included a GUI in the 1983 release of a computer called Lisa, and the 1984 release of the first Macintosh computers.

'Good artists copy, great artists steal.' Steve Jobs, quoting Pablo Picasso, when asked about stealing the GUI idea

Not Bill Gates, who included a GUI in his 1985 release of Microsoft Windows Version 1.0.

'I think it's more like we both had this rich neighbour called Xerox and I broke into his house to steal the TV set and found out that you had already stolen it.' Bill Gates, when accused by Steve Jobs of stealing the GUI idea from Apple

In fact, GUIs were dreamed up by our buddy Douglas Engelbart (the same guy who invented the computer mouse), and developed in 1973 by the team at Xerox PARC, a think tank operated by the photocopier company.

Into the future

In 1985, Steve J was asked to leave his own company. Apple had grown, and other managers disagreed with the way Steve J was behaving.

But twelve years later, he got his job back.

Ten years after that, Apple released its brand-new game-changing product. They called it the iPhone.

And ten years after that, Apple had sold more than a billion iPhones. Just how big is a billion? Well, if you talked for a billion seconds on your iPhone, you'd still be talking thirty years later ...

What would you do?

- **How do you think Steve J felt when he was basically fired from his own company? How do you think he might've channelled these feelings during the twelve years he was away? Do you think it took courage for him to return to Apple? What would you have done in the same situation?**
- **Although companies like Apple make mega-loads of cash, they don't seem to pay much tax, and taxes pay for roads, schools and hospitals. Some reports suggest Apple pays just $50 in tax for every $1,000,000 it makes. Why do you think this is? How do you feel about it?**

Bet you're wondering why there's a bull and penguin.

1983 on: Linux, Freax and freedom

Whether you're typing an email or editing a photo, you don't own the software you're using. It belongs to someone else, often the software company, and they don't want you messing with it. Not even if it helps you make better use of it.

Solution? Make your own software. Then you can do what you want with it. You can even set it free.

The tech: GNU/Linux
Invented by: Richard Stallman and Linus Torvalds

Don't tell me what to do!

Richard Matthew Stallman was never a fan of being bossed around.

'I thought of my parents as tyrants. And I resented their power.' Richard Stallman

Even at university, he rebelled. If he was locked out of a room containing a computer he needed, Richard would just crawl through the roof, lift up a bit of the ceiling, and lower down a sticky hook to pull open the door handle.

When his uni wanted everyone to password-protect their computer files, Richard rebelled. Still, they forced him to create a password.

So he made his password nothing. Literally nothing. Which meant anyone was free to read (and share) his stuff, and that was how he wanted it. Then he sent out instructions for how others could do the same.

Artificially unintelligent

Don't you just hate a paper jam? Richard did. In 1980 he was working at his uni's Artificial Intelligence lab. The lab had just been given a brand-new Xerox printer, which was great. But it kept jamming, which was a huge pain in the Xerox. People from all over the lab spent hours walking back and forth to see if their printout had worked (or partly worked) (or not worked at all).

The lab's old printer had also jammed, but Richard had

worked up an easy fix for that one: he'd added a bit of extra code to the printer's software, so that any time the printer finished a job, it would send a message to the job owner. And if it jammed, it would send a message too. Massive. Time. Saver.

So Richard set out to do the same for the Xerox machine.

Except, he wasn't allowed to. Xerox wouldn't give him the printer's software because it was a company secret, available only on a need-to-know basis. And according to Xerox, Richard didn't need to know.

That was the opposite of intelligent, Richard fumed. He knew how to solve the problem, but he wasn't free to fix it.

'I was so angry I couldn't think of a way to express it.' Richard Stallman

!!!*$%*!?

For Richard, the Xerox saga was the last straw. What was the point of having software if you weren't free to study it, improve it and share it?

'The printer incident helped me to see that non-free software was actually an injustice.' Richard Stallman

He decided things had to change.

Hey GNU! Yes, GNU

Richard began coding his own operating system in 1983. At the time, Unix was the operating system used on many university computers. A copy of Unix cost around $5000—big bickies, especially back then. But Richard's motivation was freedom, not cash.

He decided to call his new system GNU (pronounced *guh-noo*, rhymes with canoe), which is short for GNU's Not Unix*. Because his new GNU would be like Unix, but not Unix.

It was important that GNU was compatible with Unix, so Unix users could swap to GNU without hassle.

'Once GNU is written, everyone will be able to obtain good system software free, just like air ...'
Richard Stallman

***Which is short for GNU's Not Unix is Not Unix**.**
****Which is short for GNU's Not Unix is Not Unix is Not Unix***.**
*****Which is short for ... Well. You get the idea. Into infinity. GNU is a recursive acronym, which means one of its letters stands for itself.**

You can't possibly ...

Richard quit his job. He kept coding GNU. And he (slowly) recruited a team of volunteers to help him.

'People said, "Oh, this is an infinitely hard job; you can't possibly write a whole system like UNIX" ... And I said, "I'm going to do it anyway." ... I am great at being very, very stubborn.' Richard Stallman

Richard and his team nailed most of the operating system, but GNU still needed one important part: the kernel.

A kernel is software that coordinates all the other bits of software. If an operating system was an orchestra, the kernel would be the conductor: without it, nothing really works.

GNU called its kernel Hurd, and they started building it in 1990.

Richard's four freedoms

When it came to software, Richard believed* in four essential freedoms. He said you should be free:

- to run the program as you wish
- to study and change the source code as you wish
- to share copies as you wish
- to share copies of your changes as you wish.

'When we call software "free", we mean that it respects the users' essential freedoms ... think of "free speech", not "free beer".' Richard Stallman

'Everyone can sell my work. Freedom to sell copies is part of the definition of free software.' Richard Stallman

*And still believes.

Making up the rules ...

Meanwhile in Finland, in 1991, twenty-one-year-old Linus* Benedict Torvalds began writing a piece of software that would catapult him to fame.

Linus' parents were journalists and his grandfather was (you guessed it) a poet. He wrote his first programs when he was aged eleven. One code he wrote instructed his computer to compliment his sister, over and over again**:

```
Sara is the best Sara is the best Sara is the
best Sara is the best Sara is the best_
```

The more Linus mucked around, the more he loved coding.

'You get to make up your own world with its own rules.' Linus Torvalds

***Linus is pronounced LEE-nus, to rhyme with obscene-nus. Linus says he was named after the Nobel Prize winning scientist Linus Pauling, and also the thumb-sucking Linus from the *Peanuts* cartoon.**
****Yes. Brothers like this do exist.**

Hello everybody

Back to 1991: Linus was keen to buy his own PC. He used his Christmas money and organised a student loan. Then he went out and bought the best he could afford, but he was disappointed. The computer ran MS-DOS, Bill Gates' operating system, and Linus thought it was awful.

He wanted to replace MS-DOS with Unix, but the cost of

buying Unix made his eyes water.

He decided on a mini-version of Unix, called Minix, which cost a mini $169 (even that was a lot for a poor student!). Living at his mum's house, Linus began coding extras onto Minix, creating and adding his own programs and features.

Linus crowdsourced ideas (and coders) for other features ...

From: torvalds@klaava.helsinki.fi (Linus Benedict Torvalds)
To: Newsgroups: comp.os.minix
Subject: What would you like to see most in minix?
Summary: small poll for my new operating system

Hello everybody out there using minix -
I'm doing a (free) operating system (just a hobby,
won't be big and professional like gnu)

It was the summer of '91

Linus worked and built and coded and worked. He programmed all through Finland's glorious nonstop daylight summer. And by the end, he'd written 10,000 lines of code.

As his project progressed, Linus realised he wasn't just adding to Minix. He was replacing it. He'd pretty much built his own entire operating system, from scratch!

Linus wanted to call his new software something really awesome. Something killer. Something knock-your-socks-off. He had a working title, but decided instead to use the name Freax, sort of like Free-Unix.

Luckily for the world, a friend gave him some honest advice. And after that, Linus stuck with his working title: Linux. Named after himself.

Dear Linus, thanks for all the code

Although Linus hadn't yet paid off his student loan, he decided to make Linux available to the entire world, for free.

A year later, Linux was being used everywhere, and being improved and added to by thousands of coders. And it still is.

'Money is not the greatest of motivators. Folks do their best work when they are driven by passion. When they are having fun.' Linus Torvalds

Marriage

One of the communities to welcome Linux was the GNU crowd. They were still working on a GNU kernel, but without much success. And then, like an oasis in the desert, Linux appeared. Coders began working on a GNU/Linux marriage. Like a celebrity couple, the two have been appearing together ever since.

Copyleft, right?

Richard and Linus released GNU and Linux using a copyleft licence.

Copyright and copyleft can apply to all creations, including literature and art. But what's the difference? Take the example of software ...

- **Copyright** protects software on behalf of its creators: if you don't have the creator's permission, you can't use, change, share or sell the software. This software is usually proprietary, non-free software.
- **Copyleft** also protects software, but in a different way: the creator gives *everyone* permission to use, change, share or sell the software, and any changes to the software are also covered by a copyleft licence. This software is usually free.

'Proprietary software keeps the users divided and helpless, by forbidding them to share it and denying them the source code to change it. The only way I could use computers in freedom was to develop another operating system and make it free software.' Richard Stallman

Into the future

GNU/Linux now contains more than 15,000,000 lines of code, worth billions of dollars of software development time. It has been called the world's largest collaborative project.

Coders around the world still work for free to fix bugs and improve the software.

'Given enough eyeballs, all bugs are shallow.' Author and coder Eric Raymond

What would you do?

- Imagine you've spent years and years writing some software. Would you sell it for money or give it away for free? What if you'd coded a new computer game? Or a way to help people with disabilities operate their house?
- Richard believes that non-free or proprietary software can include 'back doors' that leave you open to being hacked or spied upon. He says sometimes software companies do this on purpose, in case they want information about you. Do you think this might be possible? What do you think of this idea?

PART THREE

GOING GLOBAL

1957 on: The Cold War, collaboration and Request for Comments

Just fifty years ago, computers couldn't talk to each other, or share data, or download videos from YouTube. Every computer was its own island.

Then someone came up with the idea of sharing. Because computers were expensive. And sharing is what nice people do. So in 1969, two computers across California were linked into a mini network.

Then other university computers were connected to this network.

Then this network was connected to other networks.

And then things started inter-net-working.

The tech: The internet: a twisty maze of interconnected computers, extending across the planet and beyond
Invented by: The US military, universities, and heaps more

'The Internet is really the work of a thousand people.' Paul Baran

Out-sciencing the Soviets

In the 1950s, there was a Cold War between the US and the Soviet Union*. The two nations didn't actually fight each other, but they kept threatening to, kind of like giving your sister the Silent Treatment while you're both holding loaded water pistols.

The Soviets had nuclear missiles, and intercontinental missile launchers, and—way, way worse—they also had a beach ball called Sputnik.

Sputnik wasn't actually a beach ball, it was just the size of a beach ball. It was world's first satellite. And in 1957 the Soviets launched this shiny metal in-your-face success symbol into orbit**. The US saw Sputnik as a sure sign that they were losing the race into space. They decided it was time for science.

***The Soviet Union was more properly known as the Union of Soviet Socialist Republics, and is made up of a dozen countries, including what is now Russia.**
****Sputnik orbited for three months. After that, it crashed into Earth's atmosphere and burned up completely. But it's the launch that counts.**

If your Sputnik-launching enemy is giving you the Silent Treatment while holding some really big guns, you become pretty interested in finding ways to defend yourself. So the US launched the Advanced Research Projects Agency, also known as ARPA.

It's a pretty cool beach ball.

ARPA's mission was to do really cool research that would keep the US safe and technologically brilliant (and help it catch up in the space race).

There was just one problem: ARPA had no labs or equipment. It could only work with the help of university researchers—and their computers.

You say ARPA, I say DARPA

ARPA soon changed its name to DARPA: the Defense Advanced Research Projects Agency.

One of DARPA's top dudes was Robert Taylor—you can call him Bob. Bob was doing some thinking about how to get DARPA some sweet-as computing power.

Bob's IT budget ideas

✗ **Option A: Buy speciality computers for all the researchers and all the universities.**
Cost: Are you serious? I think I need to sit down.

✓ **Option B: Figure out how to network the computers we have, and share.**
Cost: Way cheaper. But the figuring-out bit will take time ... and money.

Bob liked the way-cheaper idea, so asked his DARPA director for some cash to make it happen.

Budgeting 101: The short version

Bob: Can I have a million bucks?

Bob's boss: Sure!

Everybody in the whole world: YAY!*

***Actually, it was a military project, so everybody in the whole world didn't know about it.**

Data vs voice

Bob's team set to work inventing a way to network computers. The universities were already linked by phone lines, so that was handy, but there was one brain-straining issue:

- If you wanted to call your aunty, you made a voice call, and then you needed one phone line that stayed connected for the entire conversation.
- But what if you wanted to send data? Data is just a bunch of 1s and 0s that encodes information. How could you send it so the code didn't get mixed up? Would each bit of data need its own phone line? Would each line need to stay connected the whole time??? Things would get messy (and expensive) fast.

The researchers needed a way to send multiple data messages, all at the same time, and all using the same phone line. But how?

Divide and conquer

Many people worked on finding a way to send data efficiently. They included a UK-based bloke called Donald Davies*, a US-based bloke called Paul Baran** and another US guy named Leonard Kleinrock. They all basically came up with the same idea at the same time.

Donald called the idea 'packet switching'. Leonard called it 'queuing theory'.

Paul called it 'distributed adaptive message block switching', which was nowhere near as cool. Perhaps that's why no-one listened when Paul tried to convince the US Department of Defense to use it. He also tried to convince the phone company and the air force to use it. He even wrote *eleven* books about how it worked and how great it was. But nobody noticed.

Then, one day in 1967, the idea fell into Bob's hands.

***Donald once worked with Alan Turing on the Automatic Computing Engine (and with Klaus Fuchs, who was later found to be a Soviet spy!).**
****Paul once worked with Pres Eckert and John Mauchly on UNIVAC.**

10,000 trained mice

Packet switching works a bit like a plague of trained mice. Only instead of mice, you have data. Here's the situation:

Imagine you have 10,000 zombie mice* and a message to send to your friend. The mice line up, and you write a message across their backs. Then you ask them to scurry to your friend's house. Is it better to:

A. Ask the mice to march single-file-and-in-the-right-order

all the way to your friend's place?

or

B. Let the mice scurry to your friend's as fast as they can, then line them up again once they arrive?

Now add a traffic jam or disaster, perhaps caused by a badly timed truck (or nuclear missile).

If you go for option A, your mice will all be marching down the same street when—squeeeeak!—entire furry chunks of your message will be lost. RIP Bubbles and Mr Squeaker and thousands of their friends.**

Option B, however, is safe, flexible and fast. Even if a few mice get lost along the way, well, most of your message still arrives. And you haven't wasted time waiting for stragglers.

Now imagine that each mouse is a packet of data you're sending over phone lines. Voila! Packet switching in motion.

***Because data doesn't have a functioning brain, and neither does a zombie mouse.**
****Except of course Bubbles and Mr Squeaker are metaphorical bits of data. No mice were harmed in the making of this book.**

Put the 'inter' into internet

As well as solving tech challenges, Bob worked with people challenges. Because guess what? The university peeps weren't that keen on sharing their pride-and-joy computers. Let's face it, who likes to share?

'[They] complained they would lose computing power and said they didn't want to participate. I told them they had to, because it would let me cut my funding by a factor of three.' Bob Taylor

So because sharing is ~~caring~~ saving money, Bob (and his IT funding budget) won. The universities would be part of the new computer network, whether they liked it or not.

First cabs off the rank: University of California and the Stanford Research Institute.

Request for comments

Stephen Crocker and some fellow students were given the job of working out how to connect the University of California's computer to a fridge-sized router*.

It was an important job, so they waited for instructions. And they waited. And they waited.

'I was convinced that a corps of authority figures or grownups from Washington or Cambridge would descend at any moment and tell us what the rules were.' Stephen Crocker

But no grownups arrived, and there were no rules. So the students decided they'd work it out by themselves.

'Late one night I couldn't sleep, and the only place to work without waking people up was in the bathroom. It was 3 a.m., and I scribbled down some rules.' Stephen Crocker

These notes were used to update the team on progress. They became known as 'Request for Comments', or RFCs.

RFCs were also sent to other universities, via snail mail (no email, because no network). They let everyone know how the project was going, and also asked for people's thoughts and advice. Everyone felt involved, and loads of people chipped in with ideas.

'Hidden in the history of the RFCs is the history of human institutions for achieving cooperative work.' Vint Cerf

***Your internet connection today still relies on a router. It's a mini-computer that directs signals between different connections, and it's a vital piece of the internet's plumbing.**

Lo and behold

On 29 October 1969, the computers at the first two universities, University of California and Stanford Research Institute (over 550km apart) were connected.

On that day, the first message was sent on the brand-new network. The message was meant to be LOGIN, but the system crashed.

'Hence, the first message on the Internet was "LO", as in "Lo and behold!" We didn't plan it, but we couldn't have come up with a better message: short and prophetic.' Leonard Kleinrock

And then they were four …

The tech problems were ironed out and soon the two-computer mini-network welcomed two more computers: the University of California Santa Barbara, and the University of Utah.

The new network was named ARPANET. And it grew, and grew.

'With computer networks, the loneliness of research is supplanted by the richness of shared research.' ARPANET News, Issue 1

But the more it grew, the more it bumped into problems. For a start, different computers were set up with different technologies, much like speaking different languages. We needed a way for these technologies to interact. We needed a common language.

That's where engineers Vint Cerf and Bob Kahn came in.

Do not disturb

In 1973, Bob and Vint hired a hotel room and basically didn't leave it till they'd invented a universal way for the world's various networks to communicate. They called it TCP/IP.

The TCP/IP protocols apply to every computer on the internet. These rules spell out how packets of data (or trained-but-mindless mice) should be named and addressed:

- **TCP (Transmission Control Protocol):** instructions for putting data packets back into the right order,

and for requesting that missing packets be resent

- **IP (Internet Protocol):** instructions for how to address data packets.

Free to good home

Vint and Bob* made their invention free for everyone to use. And everyone did. Released in 1974, TCP/IP is still the internet standard today.

'It has scaled up a million times over. Not many things can do that without breaking. And yet those old protocols we created are doing just fine.' Vint Cerf

'All the world's a net! And all the data in it merely packets.' Vint Cerf

*Vint went on to become vice president at Google. Bob moved to Xerox PARC, where he helped create personal computing.

From networks to internet

ARPANET wasn't available to everyone, only to members of the ARPA-funded military cool club. Pretty soon, ARPANET was growing so fast even the military couldn't keep track of who was using it. To help keep their secrets safe, they split it into two networks: one for military stuff, the other for universities and researchers.

Meanwhile, other computer networks began to appear around the world.

Aloha, Australia

Before the internet, the most global Australian computing got was a twice-daily satellite connection from the University of Melbourne to the US Centre for Seismic Studies, set up in 1984. From that first connection, we could access the world, without a single stamp or envelope.

Australia dipped its first toe into the internet in 1989, when the University of Melbourne used TCP/IP to set up a permanent connection with the University of Hawaii. Soon other universities and CSIRO were lining up to link to the Uni of Melbourne's connection. That same year, the Australian Academic and Research Network (AARNet) was born.

Let's invent an inter-thingy

Was the internet invented for national defence, or for scientific research? Let's see how things went down:

1. The US defense department instructed US universities to invent some sort of computer network. They wanted this network to be fast, flexible and able to survive a nuclear attack. They wanted it for: NATIONAL DEFENCE
2. The universities set about agreeing on a way to connect their computers into a network. They wanted this network to encourage information sharing, cooperation and equal access. They wanted it for: COLLABORATIVE RESEARCH

The result satisfied both parties. So what's the answer? Was the internet invented for war or peace? Perhaps it depends on who you ask.

What's the difference?

- The internet is the underlying protocols and networks that connect computers together.
- The World Wide Web wasn't invented until much later; it is a file-sharing application and it needs the internet in order to work.

Into the future

Once the internet began to grow, it didn't stop. And it still hasn't ...

Today, billions of devices are connecting using the TCP/IP protocols that were developed all those years ago.

What would you do?

- Thanks to the internet, anyone can share their words, pictures or coded creations with the world. You don't need an editor's support, or your boss's permission, or even a whole lot of money to send an email or post a selfie. How do you think this has affected the world? How has it affected your life?
- The internet was developed before internet banking, before online identity theft, and before cyberbullying. If the inventors of the internet knew about these things, how do you think the internet might be different?
- An 'internaut' is an expert internet navigator. What other terms have been invented because of the internet? Can you invent some new terms of your own?

But wait! Didn't Al Gore invent the internet?

Uh, no.

The idea that US politician Al Gore invented the internet has become a bit of a joke. He didn't. But he did help a bit with the World Wide Web. Remind me to tell you some more about that later.

No, he didn't invent the internet (nor did he ever claim to have done so).

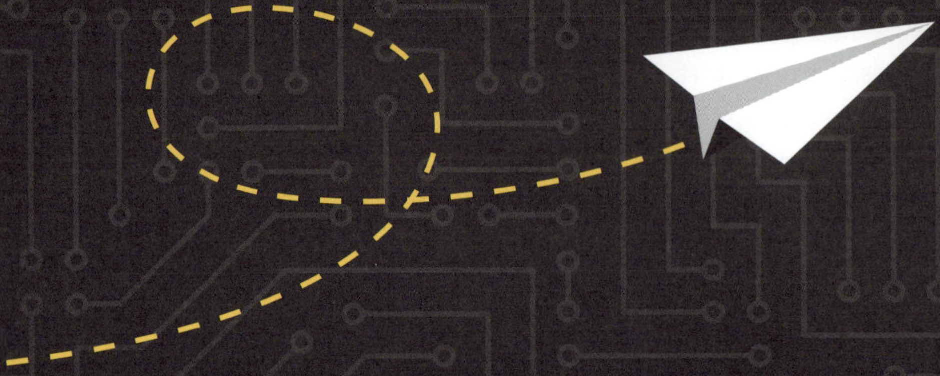

1965 on: Email, emoticons and @

Imagine you have the power of a dozen computers at your fingertips. You could calculate the weather, design an aircraft, simulate a rocket launch ...

What do you do? You message your friends. Because humans are driven to communicate. And almost as soon as we figured out how to network computers, we started sending emails.

The tech: Electronic mail
Invented by: Ray Tomlinson

SNDMSG

Before email, there was SNDMSG.
This stood for:

a) Sound Massage
b) Sand Misguided
c) Send Message
d) Don't know

Answer: C

Here's how it worked: If you and your buddy both had personal mailboxes on the same computer, you could use SNDMSG to pass electronic notes between you.

Your mailbox was just a long file of plain text. If you received new mail, the computer would paste it onto the bottom of your mailbox file.

But SNDMSG didn't work if you and your mate were on different computers. If that happened, you had to go for hand delivery, post or carrier pigeon.

CPYNET

Ray Tomlinson worked as a programmer, and he'd created CPYNET, an experimental program that could send files from one networked computer to another.

CPYNET stood for:

a) Spy Net
b) Cents. Pence. Yen. Extra-terrestrial.
c) Copy Network
d) No idea. If you know, please write in and tell us.

Answer: D

Since CPYNET could send *files* through the network, with a bit of tinkering, perhaps it could also send messages. So Ray combined it with SNDMSG.

@ last

To address the messages clearly and avoid confusion, Ray needed something to separate the sender's name from their computer's name. The symbol couldn't be a space, and it couldn't be part of any name.

He needed an unloved symbol. A symbol with no real purpose. A symbol just wasting space on the keyboard.

His eyes fell upon @. & it was ❤ @ first sight. Till then, @ had only been used to multiply things:

- 5 kg of oranges @ $2/kg
- 10 lollipops @ $1.50 each

But Ray rescued @, and now it's one of the most recognised symbols in any language anywhere in the world. And it's still used to separate the two names: username@hostname

You've got mail!

No joke: Ray *emailed* his friends to let them know he'd invented email.

But his first messages didn't win any prizes for literature:

'The test messages were entirely forgettable and I have, therefore, forgotten them. Most likely the first message was QWERTYUIOP or something similar.' Ray Tomlinson

The other cheek

Email was fast, but it could be confusing. How could you tell if someone was joking? Or being sarcastic?

To help out, in 1979, Kevin MacKenzie suggested using a 'tongue-in-cheek' symbol to show that you were joking.

-)

It wasn't long till people turned Kevin's cheek into a smile.

19-Sep-82 11:44 Scott E Fahlman :-)
From: Scott E Fahlman <Fahlman at Cmu-20c>

I propose that the following character sequence for joke markers: :-)
Read it sideways. Actually, it is probably more economical to mark things that are NOT jokes, given current trends. For this, use :-(

And beyond!

:-p :-D :-/ :-o ;-) }:-) >:/ :-L

:-X :'-(|;-) >;) :-|| DX

(>_<) O_O O_o

(͡° ͜ʖ ͡°)

Into the future

Email went from strength to strength as other coders added to it. Soon there was a proper inbox, with mail you could open, archive, forward and even delete. Later you could email links, images, videos, birthday cards and more ...

Today email is loads more popular (and a zillion times faster) than stamp-and-envelope mail. There are billions of email accounts in the world, sending even more billions of emails, much of them spam. Perhaps like 'QWERTYUIOP' or something similar.

What would you do?

- When Ray chose @ for addressing email, he helped us think of the internet as a place. You can be @ the beach, or @ the park, or @ an email address. What if he'd picked a different symbol, like * or ^? Do you think it might've changed the way we think about the internet?
- Early email programs had no function for replying to emails, or putting emails in order, or displaying emails in any sort of menu or inbox. These things were invented as people realised just how useful they were. What new email function do you think would be useful? What function would you like to invent?

1980s on: Cow-feeders, slot machines and ARM processors

Back when smartphones were still sci-fi dreams and desktop computers occupied your whole table, two people invented a microchip that changed the world.

The tech: **More than 50 billion ARM processors: ARM stands for Advanced RISC Machine, and RISC stands for Reduced Instruction Set Computing. And WT? stands for confused. So read on, and let's try to simplify things (because simplify is what ARM processors do best).**

Invented by: **Sophie Wilson and Steve Furber**

Mooo-vellous!

Sophie Wilson studied maths at uni, but 'failed quite badly' (according to her), so she switched to computing.

Over the Easter holidays, instead of studying, like she was supposed to, she scored an odd-job for a farmer. Her aim? To build an automatic cow-feeder. She ordered some cheap microchips from the US, and bingo! Happy cows.

You're a winner! Again! And again!

Later, Sophie scored another job: her boss set her to work solving a problem in the gambling industry. Electronic slot machines had become the Next Big Thing. Punters would feed their coins into the machine, pull the handle, and watch the images spin, hoping for a win. Three cherries in a row and your winnings would automatically flow from the machine.

The problem was newfangled cigarette lighters. These lighters worked by sparking a 1000-volt pulse of energy. If you sparked the slot machine instead of your cigarette, you could trick the machine into awarding you win after win after win. Talk about getting rich quick!

Sophie's job was to stop the cigarette cheats. Too easy. She came up with a super-simple solution. She designed a radio receiver that sat inside each slot machine. If the receiver detected an electromagnetic pulse, the machine would not pay out.

Turns out finding simple solutions was what Sophie did best.

A million acorns

Sophie's next challenge again came from her bossy boss: this time he dared her to build a cheap personal computer by the end of her summer holidays.

So she did.

Sophie used the same microchips she'd used in the cow-feeder. The PC she built was—surprise—simple. They called it the Acorn System One and sold it for just 70 pounds (around $120). Her boss hoped to sell 12,000. Instead, they sold more than a million.

Acorn Computers was born!

BBC Micro

Hot on the heels of Acorn 1, Sophie and her co-worker Steve Furber created an 8-bit microcomputer called the BBC Micro for the British Broadcasting Corporation (the same BBC that do BBC TV). Sophie managed the entire project, designing a microcomputer and coding its operating system (they called it BBC BASIC).

On a crazy deadline for the BBC, their first design took less than a week. For the rest of the summer, they worked on improving it.

The BBC was happy, but Sophie knew she could make it better, faster and simpler.

RISCy business

Around the same time, hardware giant IBM was trying a new concept: RISC, which stood for Reduced Instruction Set Computing. But although RISC was designed to make things simpler, IBM couldn't get it right. And neither could anyone else.

Except Sophie. She worked out most of the problems in her head, inventing a nifty chip that became the brain of BBC Micros. She and Steve called the processor ARM, for Acorn RISC Machine.

'Sophie did it all in her brain.' Herman Hauser, Sophie Wilson's boss

'While Intel and Motorola and all these universities had money and resources, Herman gave us something that they didn't—no money and no resources—we had to keep things simple.' Sophie Wilson

Keeping it simple

ARM processors went on to blow people's minds. They were loads faster, needed five times fewer transistors, and used so little energy that the first time Sophie and Steve switched it on, they thought it was broken.

The secret to success? Again, it was simplicity.

Ordinary microchips came with hundreds of instructions, from the incredibly basic to the staggeringly complex.

Just like words in the English language, some instructions were used over and again (like 'the', 'at' or 'is'), and others were hardly used at all (like 'antidisestablishmentarianism' and 'Brobdingnagian'*).

Sophie's ARM processor cut out the complicated, rarely used instructions and kept the rest. If she wanted the computer to do something tricky, she replaced one complicated instruction with a series of basic instructions. The result was a much faster chip.

She also designed the chip so instructions arrived and were processed one after the other, all in a rapid row. Other chips were S L O W, fetching and processing each instruction separately.

There were very few of us designing the first ARM, so we couldn't make a complicated processor.'
Sophie Wilson

***I totally love this word (it means 'gigantic', BTW). I dare you to use it in a sentence by the end of the week.**

ARMs race

Meanwhile, Acorn Computers was slowly going broke. No-one was buying Acorn computers, but everyone loved ARM chips.

So Acorn and Apple Computers joined forces to make a new company: ARM. This company still licenses the ARM processors in your smartphones and tablets today.

Element 14

Sophie left Acorn, and in the 1990s, she started a new company, Element 14*.

She also developed a new processor, called FirePath, which is still used in many broadband networks. In 2001, Sophie sold the company for $594 million.

All up, Sophie's inventions have earned more than $30 billion dollars—and that's only so far.

***Element 14. Geddit? Geddit? It's what most modern processors and microchips are made from. Don't geddit? Go check your periodic table. Or think of a famous valley.**

Size matters

Back when Sophie and Steve invented the ARM processor, size didn't matter. The most important thing was that it worked. But as devices became smaller and smaller, teeny-tiny, uber-efficient microprocessors became more and more vital.

Today, the microprocessors in your smartphone, your digital TV, and even your smart fridge, are descended from that first ARM.

Into the future

Take the number of people on this planet and multiply that by seven. That's how many ARM processors have been created.

'We wanted to produce a processor used by everybody, and so we have.' Sophie Wilson

Today's ARM chips are faster than Sophie's original, and 10,000 times smaller, but they still use the same logic. Upwards of five billion ARM chips are created every year.

'In 2008 we hit the point where ten billion cores had been sold and me and Steve looked at each other and said "that's pretty strange—more than one for every person on the planet". But it's gone past being weird. The numbers are so insane.' Sophie Wilson

What would you do?

- **Sophie thinks Acorn Computers went broke because it wasn't good at marketing its computers. Design a poster that promotes the benefits of buying an Acorn Computer.**
- **The first ARM used so little power that Sophie and Steve thought it wasn't working at all, but it turned out they'd accidentally created a super-efficient chip. These happy accidents, where researchers discover something they didn't actually set out to discover, happen more often than you'd think. Research some other serendipitous discoveries. Choose one and draw a comic describing what happened.**

1989 on: HTTP, WWW and TBL

How many facts can you remember? A hundred? A million? A hundred million? There's so much going on in the world, it's impossible for one person to know it all, let alone keep all that information organised and catalogued.

Luckily, we have an amazing way of sharing the world's information, and it's right at our fingertips.

The tech: The World Wide Web
Invented by: Tim Berners-Lee (TBL to his fans)

World Wide what?

Before the World Wide Web, if you wanted information, you had to find it in a book (but first you had to find the right book), or ask your neighbour (but first you had to find the right neighbour).

'Hey, what's the life cycle of a flea?'

'...'

'Hey, who won the 1999 Premiership?'

'...'

'Hey, where can I find an intelligent neighbour?'

'...'

Waste not, want not

As a kid, Tim Berners-Lee loved his train set. He started building electronics to control the trains. Then he realised he loved electronics more than trains.

Both of Tim's parents were computer programmers, so he grew up surrounded by computer talk. One day he even built himself a computer out of a broken TV.

Help! Hilf! Aidez-moi!

After studying physics at uni, Tim did a six-month stint at CERN, the European Organization for Nuclear Research*.

Tim quickly realised that CERN needed help. There were thousands of scientists working on dozens of projects, all on separate computers, and often speaking different languages (the people *and* the computers).

There was no easy way to share data or ideas.

So in 1980, Tim created a computer program that linked CERN's different people and projects. He called it ENQUIRE, named for an encyclopaedia he'd loved as a kid: *Enquire Within Upon Everything.*

But then Tim's time at CERN was up. He left. His computer was given to someone else. His code disappeared.

Enquire Within as much as you like, but ENQUIRE was gone.

***The nuclear bit has nothing to do with nuclear weapons. CERN is focused on nuclei: the teensy-tiny stuff at the centre of atoms. CERN uses the infinitesimally small to learn about the mind-blowingly large: our universe. Scientists still flock from all over the world to CERN, working for the chance to see deep inside the smallest packages on Earth atoms to find smaller particles neutrons and protons and hopefully glimpse even tinier packages subatomic particles with names like lepton, boson, gluon and bottom quark (not to be confused with other, smellier bottom quarks you might be more familiar with).**

The World Wide Tree

Tim wasn't the first person to try organising the internet's information. Most internet fans were obsessed with making lists. These lists worked like trees: they had a central trunk, with different topics branching off into more and more detailed topics.

But information doesn't always link like branches in a tree ...

... Sometimes, it's more like strands in a web.

'Suppose all the information stored on computers everywhere were linked. There would be a single global information space. A web of information would form.' Tim Berners-Lee

'Vague, but exciting'

Lucky for us (and for the Instafamous everywhere), Tim returned to CERN. He decided to rebuild ENQUIRE, bigger and better than before. He called it Tangle. Less like a tree. More like a web. Or a sandpit.

'I wanted to build a creative space, something like a sandpit where everyone could play together.' Tim Berners-Lee

Tim wrote his sandpit/web idea into a proposal. In March 1989, he showed it to his boss, Mike Sendall, but Mike didn't really get it.

'When I read Tim's proposal, I could not figure out what it was, but I thought it was great.' Mike Sendall

So, Mike wrote just three words on the top of Tim's paper:

'Vague, but exciting.'

Which sort of translates to: 'Don't get it. Wa-hey!'

Luckily, Tim wasn't put off by Mike's equally vague response. He didn't wait for official permission. He just kept working on his idea. And working, and working.

Dub dub dub

Tim had called his proposal 'Information Management'. His co-worker, Robert Cailliau, pointed out that this was incredibly boring. So Robert worked with Tim to find something a little less ... vague.

Ideas:

- **Mine Of Information (MOI) -> No good! 'Moi' means 'Me' in French. You sound like an egomaniac!**
- **The Information Mine (TIM) -> No good! You still sound like an egomaniac!**
- **World Wide Web (WWW) -> No good! The acronym takes longer to say than the name!**

But Tim liked the sound of World Wide Web. He thought it had a nice ring to it.

Merry Christmas!

Tim set about creating what soon became the World Wide Web. He coded the first web browser—software to help people surf web pages. And he wrote three epic sets of webby rules:

- **HTML:** Hypertext Markup Language, for how information should be structured on a page.
- **HTTP:** Hypertext Transfer Protocol, for how computers can access information from other computers.

- **UDI:** Universal Document Identifier*, for naming web pages.

The code took Tim just three months to write, but it's still the bee's knees of the web today.

Finally, in November 1990, CERN officially approved Tim's proposal. He was ready! Tim and Robert had the tech up and running by Christmas Day. The World Wide Web was born!**

*Never heard of a UDI? That's because Tim changed the name. People thought 'universal' was a bit too hopeful. (As if this crazy web idea would ever be that popular! Ha!) So Tim changed 'Universal' to 'Uniform'. He also changed 'Document' to 'Resource', which was handy, because today's web is about loads more than just documents. And 'Identifier' became 'Locator'. Voila! UDI became URL.

**About a week later, Tim's first child was born, too.

Note: Tim is not actually a spider.

Why www?

A URL is a list of instructions for where to find a resource. As the web grew, many people included the prefix 'www' at the front of their URL, to indicate that the resource was a web page. These days, since most of us are looking for web pages when we surf the net, the 'www' bit is often left off.

Mail me

But the web wasn't an overnight success. Tim and his pals worked hard for years to spread the word.

From: timbl@info.cern.ch
Subject: Re: Qualifiers on Hypertext links …
Date: 6 Aug 91 14:56:20 GMT
The WorldWideWeb project aims to allow links to be made to any information anywhere …
If you're interested in using the code, mail me.
It's very prototype …
Collaborators welcome!

Free to a billion good homes

The web was about free communication, and Tim wanted his inventions and code to be free for anyone to use. CERN agreed. In 1993 they released Tim's code for free.

Gopher broke

The web wasn't the only system invented to manage information on the internet.

One competitor, called Gopher, worked by organising information into folders. But Tim's web could read Gopher pages, and soon users had to pay for Gopher, while the World Wide Web was free ...

Other competitors, like Microsoft's private network, MSN, saw the writing on the webby wall and quickly developed their own WWW pages.

The web is now part of our ordinary life. But it's still changing and growing ...

'If we want a Web that is truly for everyone, then everyone must play a role in shaping its next 25 years.' Tim Berners-Lee in 2014, on the Web's 25th birthday

Into the future

'Here is my hope.

The Web is a tool for communicating.

With the Web, you can find out what other people mean. You can find out where they are coming from.

The Web can help people understand each other.

Think about most of the bad things that have happened between people in your life. Maybe most of them come down to one person not understanding another. Even wars.

Let's use the Web to create neat new exciting things.

Let's use the Web to help people understand each other.' Tim Berners-Lee

'I want you to know that you too can make new programs which create new fun ways of using computers and using the Internet.

I want you to realize that, if you can imagine a computer doing something, you can program a computer to do that.

Unbounded opportunity ... limited only by your imagination.' Tim Berners-Lee

What would you do?

- Tim was born in 1955, the same year as Bill Gates and Steve Jobs. Back then you could buy electronic parts and build circuits at home. Do you think Tim was just in the right place at the right time?
- Tim wasn't the first person to come up with hyperlinks. As far back as the 1950s Ted Nelson was experimenting with hypertext. Ted wanted to use two-way links, so both pages had to agree to be linked. Tim's web uses just one-way linking, so you can link to anything, without permission. How do you think the web would be different if we needed agreement before making a link? How might it be better? How might it be worse?
- The web was built on trust, designed to be totally open and totally free. Unfortunately, that means it's also open to trolls, spammers and spreaders of fake news. What's the best way to regulate these sorts of behaviours?
- Tim works for the World Wide Web Consortium, trying to 'unlock the web's untapped potential'. How do you think the web could be further improved?

But wait! Weren't you going to tell me about Al Gore not inventing the internet?

Oh yeah.

So, Al didn't invent the net, but he did help spread the word. He was US Vice President when the World Wide Web was still finding its feet. Al did loads of things to promote the spread of WWW: he funded the WWW Consortium, he made the White House create a website using WWW tech (they had been using Gopher), and he funded the creation of Mosaic, the first madly popular user-friendly web browser.

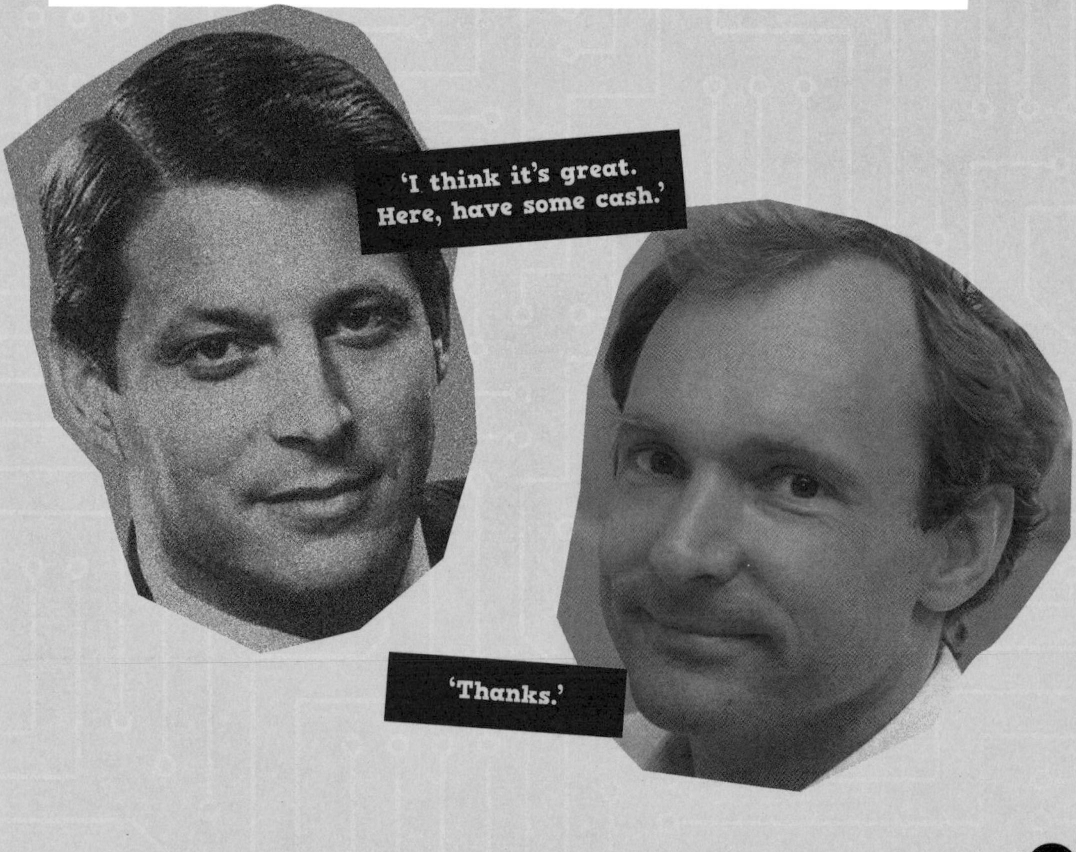

1990s on: Black holes, sohcE and a speedy solution

If you're using the internet without plugging in a cable, you're on wi-fi.

Wi-fi is the through-thin-air technology that links our devices without using wires. It was invented by a team from Australia's CSIRO.

The tech: Fast and reliable Wireless Local Area Networks (WLANs), also known as wi-fi
Invented by: John O'Sullivan and his team of CSIRO radio astronomers: Diet Ostry, Graham Daniels, John Deane and Terry Percival

Black hole detectives

As a kid, John O'Sullivan wasn't really sure what he wanted to do, but he knew he liked science.

'My mum used to bring home books from the library and I read everything I could get my hands on about the astronauts.' John O'Sullivan

Then one day his school visited Sydney University, and curiosity ruled.

'There was one simple experiment there, a spinning disc with a magnet across it generating an electric current, and I couldn't for the life of me see how it worked, but I thought it was wonderful.' John O'Sullivan

John decided to study radio astronomy and was soon searching for evaporating black holes.

'The black holes we're talking about might weigh as much as Everest but are the size of an atomic particle.' John O'Sullivan

If you've never searched for an evaporating black hole before, you might not know that one of the best clues for finding a monstrous light-gobbling space-and-time-bending black hole billions of kilometres away is ... radio waves.

Radio waves are not radios

Radio waves are a form of electromagnetic energy. Light is also a form of electromagnetic energy. If you take a few wavelengths of red light and stretch them out, you get infrared light, and if you stretch out infrared light, you get microwaves, and if you give microwaves a super-stretchy stretch, you get the super-long-wavelength waves we call radio waves.

On Earth, we use radio waves to send coded information to devices like walkie-talkies, mobile phones and … radios. Radios make soundwaves by decoding the radio waves that are broadcast by radio stations. But radio waves have nothing to do with sound. And if you see the word radio too often, it looks strange. Radio. Radio. Radio.

Back to black holes …

Just as you can pinpoint a torch by tracking the light energy that shines from it, radio astronomers can find objects in space by observing the energy they produce.

But if you're trying to find a black hole, you can run into trouble: black holes have so much gravity that even light cannot escape their clutches.

But sometimes, gas clouds near a black hole will spit out X-rays that bounce into other gas clouds, then turn into radio waves.

And these radio waves travel across space and time to reach Earth. Score!

Echo ohcE

But what happens, after years and years of travelling through space, when your precious radio waves finally arrive?

They bounce. Off walls, off books, off coffee mugs, off your face. And they all bounce in different ways and at different times. So by the time they bounce into your signal collector, there are multiple multiple multiple multiple multiple copies of the same signal, all mixed up with other other other other other signals.

They order arrive arrive arrive in wrong the.

Or echo they ohce echo ohce.

Or reverberate. Rebertaverb.

Which makes it nearly impossible to learn anything sensible about they from came where. What?

To have a chance of tracking the bouncing radio waves to the black holes that may have spawned them, John's team needed a way to create order from the chaos.

Recipe for success

Meanwhile on Earth, researchers were facing the same bounce-and-echo problem with wireless networking.

In wireless networking, we use radio waves to send coded messages. Because of all the bouncing around, it helps to break the message into smaller parts. You can try this in loads of ways: by sending different parts on different waves, or sending the same parts in a different order, or sending different parts multiple times.

Each of these ideas was decades old—and soooo slow. But

the CSIRO team wanted to build something WAY FASTER! They began experimenting with new ways of using existing techniques.

'We had those concepts, but we had to work out how to glue them together ... you had to fine tune and adjust to make sure you got the best possible performance out of the system.' Terry Percival

Using trial and error and loads of tests, the team worked on different ways of combining these ideas. Eventually, they came up with a fast, efficient, sweet-as solution for untangling a mess of radio waves.

'Back when we first started thinking about this, there were networks, but they were 50 or 100 times slower than what we were trying to do. One of the parts of our solution was to send a whole lot of bits on different frequencies at a slower rate.' John O'Sullivan

The team's aim was to find a way to unscramble radio waves from outer space. Along the way, they found a way to do the same thing on Earth.

By using the CSIRO solution, you could create order from wireless chaos. Wi-fi was born—only they didn't call it that yet.

If at first you don't succeed ...

John's team tried to sell its solution to big tech companies, including Apple and Hewlett-Packard. No-one was buying.

'One of the large companies even said: "Oh, look, wireless, that's a passing fad".' Terry Percival

Then in 2002, several companies started selling electronic devices that used the CSIRO solution ... without CSIRO's permission.

CSIRO took these companies to court, asking that they pay to use its technology. In 2007, CSIRO won. The companies paid $220 million in fees.

In all, CSIRO earned more than $400 million from the team's discoveries.

Why wi-fi?

CSIRO's technology was used in the standard international specifications for wireless local area networks (WLANs), developed by the Institute of Electrical and Electronics Engineers (IEEE) and known as IEEE 802.11. This is clearly a catchy name. Not.

Luckily, back in the '90s, the peeps at the Wireless Ethernet Compatibility Alliance (WECA) decided they needed a better name.

They employed some marketing gurus to invent a new

name, and wi-fi was the winner. It's not an acronym, and it doesn't stand for anything. But it rhymes with hi-fi, which makes it cool.

So WECA became the Wi-Fi Alliance. And the world became wi-fi-enabled.

Into the future

John won the 2009 Prime Minister's Award for Science. The wireless technology John's team invented is used every day in billions of electronic devices—printers, phones, tablets and more—all over the world. We now have more wi-fi devices than people.

What would you do?

- Although John's team invented wi-fi, they didn't find a single evaporating black hole. Do you think their story is one of failure, or success?
- Do you think it's important to know what you're trying to invent when you start inventing? Or is it enough to be open to the new ideas you find as you go along?
- Wi-fi means you don't need a desk to do your job anymore. You can work from the beach, from the treetops, from the bus or from your bike. But most people still commute to a central office. Why do you think this is? Where would you most love to work?

PART FOUR
DOING SOCIAL

1995 on: Backrub, blue carpet and a googol of doodles

As the Web began to spread, tangle and grow, loads of people tried to invent clever ways to surf their way through it. Most of these search engines worked by counting how many times a word appeared on a shipwreck cheese recipe Brad Pitt website.

But just because a website includes a certain zebra astronaut handbag lamington keyword doesn't mean the website is actually relevant to that insert-keyword-here. So how can you work out which websites are actually useful?

Thankfully, back in the '90s, two students began working on Backrub ...

The tech: Google
Started by: Larry Page and Sergey Brin

'Larry Page'

- received his first computer when he was six years old
- played saxophone and studied computer science
- built a working inkjet printer out of Lego when he was at uni
- was part of his uni's solar car team
- speaks in a semi-whisper because of damaged vocal cords

'Sergey Brin'

- left Russia for the US when he was six years old
- finished high school in just three years
- studied maths and computer science, when he wasn't sailing, skiing or scuba diving
- returned to Russia for a school trip and threw pebbles at a police car ... narrowly escaping big-time police-type trouble
- loves skydiving and can walk on his hands

Obnoxious^2

When Larry joined Stanford University in 1995, Sergey was already a second-year student. Sergey had volunteered to show the newbies around, including Larry. It wasn't exactly love at first sight.

'I thought he was pretty obnoxious. He had really strong opinions about things, and I guess I did, too.' Larry Page

'We both found each other obnoxious.' Sergey Brin

Sergey and Larry argued for nearly the whole tour—but they kind of liked it.

Fun with backlinks

Larry was at uni to complete a big research project, but he needed to choose a topic. He liked maths, so decided he'd work out the mathematical structure of the World Wide Web. Because why not? It seemed a fun mystery. The web was sewn together with links, but where did all those links go? And what shape did they make?

Larry figured there were two kinds of links on a webpage:

1. Links leading *away from* the page (easy to research: just click on each link and see where it takes you)
2. Links leading *to* the page, called backlinks (way trickier to research: you'd have to trawl the entire web to see which links were pointing to you)

You could include a zillion links on your webpage, but that didn't mean your page was useful.

But if you had a zillion *backlinks* pointing to your page ... Well, that showed that at least someone thought your page was useful. And if those backlinks came from other useful pages, then it showed that someone useful thought your page was useful. Larry realised that would be useful.

So he decided to focus on backlinks. He called his project Backrub.

You rub my back ...

Sergey heard about Backrub and wanted to join in. He had some crazy maths skills, and by now he and Larry had stopped pretending to be frenemies and were proper friends (though they still liked arguing).

Larry and Sergey turned their research into a new kind of search engine. They called it a 'web crawler'. It didn't rely on keywords. Instead, it searched out and counted how many backlinks websites had. It also measured whether those backlinks came from useful sites.

Sounds easy? It was exponentially difficult. This is how it worked:

1. Choose one website.
2. Find out how many websites include backlinks that point to that website.
3. Find out how many websites include backlinks that point to each of the websites that backlinked to the first website.
4. Find out how many websites include backlinks that point to each of the websites that backlinked to the websites that backlinked to the first website ...
5. ... etc.

The idea was simple. Making it happen was a brainspin. So was ~~begging for~~ acquiring the masses of computers required to crunch the numbers.

'At Stanford [University] we'd stand on the loading dock and try to snag computers as they came in. We would see who got 20 computers and ask them if they could spare one.' Larry Page

Google a googol

The search engine was still called Backrub, but the pair wanted something better. Something … bigger. They came up with Google!*

The word google is a misspelling of the number googol, which is a maths joke** about the seemingly infinite amount of information in the world.

- One thousand: 1 followed by 3 zeroes: 1000
- One million: 1 followed by 6 zeroes: 1,000,000
- One googol: 1 followed by 100 zeroes: 10,000,000,000,000,000,000,000,000,000,000,000,000,000,000,000,000,000,000,000,000,000,000,000,000,000,000,000,000,000,000,000,000,000,000,000,000

***Yes! That's right! Google! It included an exclamation mark!**
****They do exist.**

00000000000000000000
00000000000000000000
00000000000000000000
00000000000000000000
00000000000000000000

The zeroes in a googol.

There are 10^{4229} googols printed on the background of these two pages (including the 0s hidden behind the text boxes). Just so we're clear about how big a googol is, there are an estimated 10^{80} particles in the known universe. A googol is 10^{100}.

Cha-ching!

By 1998, Larry and Sergey were running the Google search engine from their dorm rooms at university. Then their first investor signed a cheque for $100,000. Ka-ching! They'd hit the big time!

They celebrated by moving to a new and uber-flash Google HQ: a friend's empty garage*, complete with bright blue carpet, a ping-pong table, and Yoshka**, an oversized extra-hairy dog.

***The garage belonged to Susan Wojcicki, Larry and Sergey's sixteenth employee. Susan went on to become the CEO of YouTube.**
****Yoshka belonged to Urs Hölzle, Larry and Sergey's eighth employee. Yoshka was a Leonberger (from Germany).**

Burning doodle

Google is famous for the doodles that appear on its homepage each day. Each doodle celebrates a (usually) serious and meaningful event. Seriously.

But the first doodle wasn't a celebration, just an out-of-office message. The entire Google staff had taken a break and headed out to Burning Man, a huge arts festival in the Nevada desert. They inserted the Burning Man logo behind Google's second 'o' ... and a tradition was born.

LarryRank

PageRank is the mathematical algorithm that Google uses to work out how important each website is. Is it named after webpages? Or Larry?

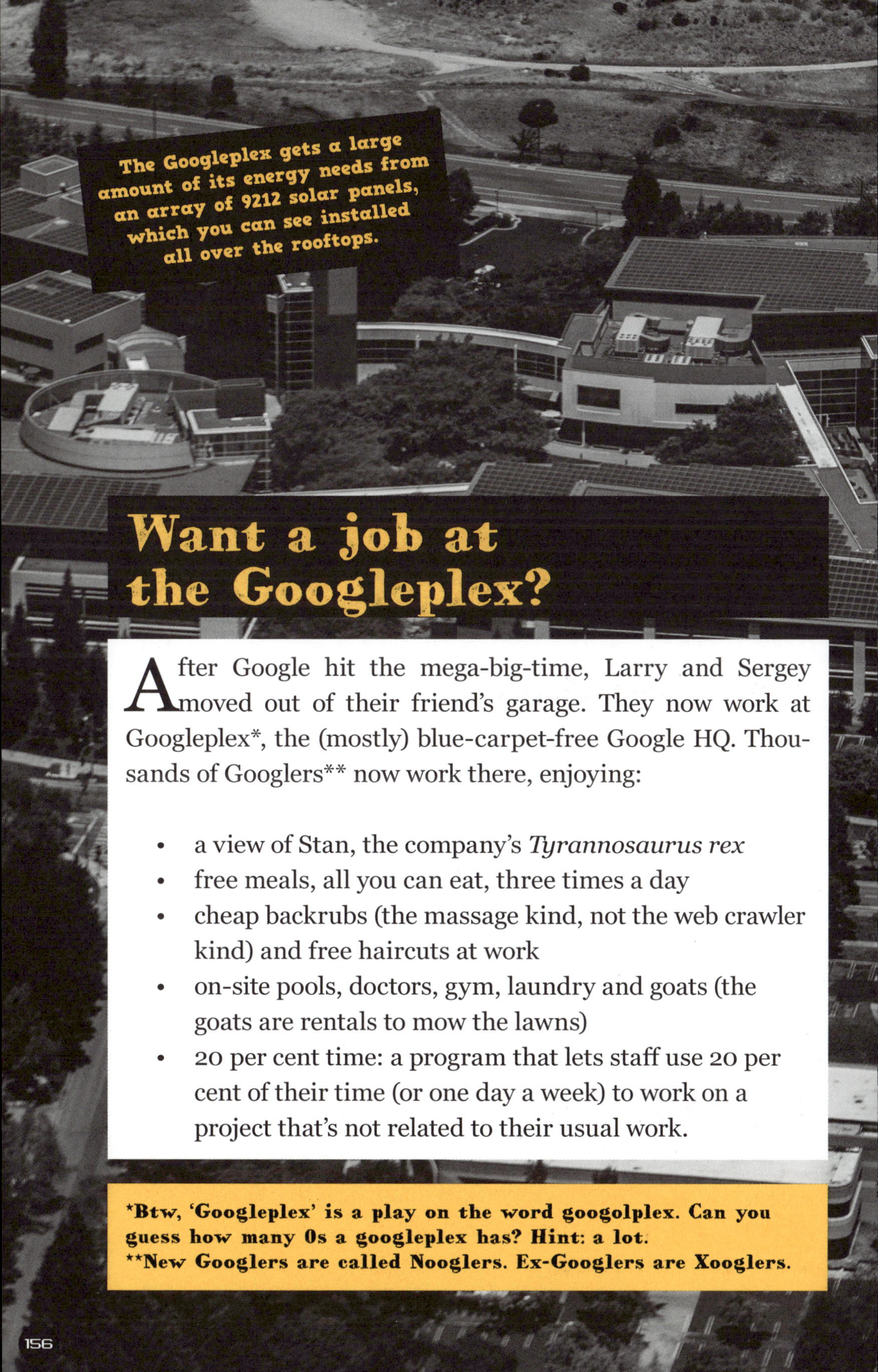

The Googleplex gets a large amount of its energy needs from an array of 9212 solar panels, which you can see installed all over the rooftops.

Want a job at the Googleplex?

After Google hit the mega-big-time, Larry and Sergey moved out of their friend's garage. They now work at Googleplex*, the (mostly) blue-carpet-free Google HQ. Thousands of Googlers** now work there, enjoying:

- a view of Stan, the company's *Tyrannosaurus rex*
- free meals, all you can eat, three times a day
- cheap backrubs (the massage kind, not the web crawler kind) and free haircuts at work
- on-site pools, doctors, gym, laundry and goats (the goats are rentals to mow the lawns)
- 20 per cent time: a program that lets staff use 20 per cent of their time (or one day a week) to work on a project that's not related to their usual work.

***Btw, 'Googleplex' is a play on the word googolplex. Can you guess how many 0s a googleplex has? Hint: a lot.**
****New Googlers are called Nooglers. Ex-Googlers are Xooglers.**

Mission (impossible?):

Google says its mission is 'to organise the world's information and make it universally accessible and useful'. Too easy!

So far, to achieve this mission, Google has:

- stored more than 100 million gigabytes of data in its search index. (Imagine 100,000 one-terabyte drives and you're there)
- driven down (and photographed) millions of kilometres of road, all over the world, for Google Street View
- achieved 100 per cent renewable energy, including wind and solar energy, to power their data centres and offices.

Whoops!

Once, on 19 August 2013, Google's services dropped out for five minutes. During this time, traffic across the entire web dropped by 40 per cent.

Cool-gle

Google prides itself on being unconventional, which means there's always some fun to be had. Try googling for:

- 'Google Mars'—and explore the surface of our favourite red planet
- 'askew'—but be prepared to tilt your neck

- 'Atari Breakout' in Google Images—and see if you can beat your own best score
- 'Zerg rush'—can you destroy the swarming aliens before they eat your search results?

g is for alphabet

In 2015, Larry and Sergey invented Alphabet, a new umbrella company that includes Google and a bunch of other Google-owned companies.

Some people estimate that Alphabet buys one new company every week. Here are just a few things that Alphabet owns:

- YouTube
- Android
- (a large part of) HTC
- Feedburner
- Blogger
- Picasa
- X lab
- Wing
- Oyster
- Apigee
- Kaggle
- Bitium
- Skybox imaging
- reCAPTCHA (more on this one soon)

Into the future

Google has moved way beyond a search engine. Today the company spends loads of money programming driverless cars, researching ways to live longer, and teaching machines to think.

Larry and Sergey are creating eyeglasses that can see, hear and react to your world, and computers so smart they can decide when they want to interact with you, instead of the other way around.

Google continues to earn billions of dollars each month by selling ads that it shows on webpages. The ads are personalised, because Google collects information about its users, including what you do when you're online, and where you might like to spend your money.

What would you do?

- Google only works because Tim Berners-Lee designed the web to use one-way linking: you can link to anyone without letting them know. If you remember, Ted Nelson's idea was to use two-way links, so that both webmasters had to agree before their pages could be linked. If we'd gone with Ted's web, how do you think Google would be different?
- Imagine you're an insanely rich computer entrepreneur. Now imagine you want to spend a wad of cash on a new project. What would you choose? A new gadget? A new technology? Sketch out your project and what it will do.
- When you hide a joke or secret message in an ordinary program, it's called an Easter Egg. What Easter Egg would you program into the Google homepage? Swarming aliens? A tilt?

2000 on: Turing tests, old books and Games With A Purpose

How many hours every week do you spend playing computer games? Now multiply that by every person in the world who plays computer games.

What if you all worked together? What if all that time could somehow be put to good use? And what if it was loads of fun?

The tech: Games With A Purpose
Invented by: Luis von Ahn

Luis von Ahn grew up in Spanish-speaking Guatemala, South America. He was eight years old when his mum gave him his first computer: a Commodore 64. Straightaway, he was into it, teaching himself how to program games.

Called 'hyperactive' as a kid, Luis loved to work for just seven minutes, then jump up to walk around and think, then sit back down for another seven minutes.

Human computation

'Together we're the biggest supercomputer in the world.' Luis von Ahn

Luis is big into human computation: harnessing a small bit of everyone's brain to achieve something huge, often involving computers.

'It's just taking something that people do anyways and trying to extract value out of it.' Luis von Ahn

Free gym membership!

When Luis was twelve years old, he had one of his first big ideas: why not attach generators to running machines, so when people worked out at the gym, they could make electricity at the same time!?!

Even better, you could make gym membership free, so heaps of people would come to work out, and then you could

sell the electricity those people make!?! OMG! What could possibly go wrong?

Um. Laziness?

'It turns out it's not a very good idea. People aren't very good at generating electricity. It's much better to charge a membership fee.' Luis von Ahn

But Luis didn't give up.

Prove you're a human!

When Luis was at uni, the world was drowning in spam. The spammers worked like this:

1. Write a program that signed up for hundreds and thousands of free email accounts.
2. Write another program that used those email accounts to send out millions of spam emails.

Luis wanted to stop the spam. He needed a quick and easy test that humans could pass and computers would fail.

Cat-dog-cat.jpg

To develop the anti-spam test, Luis needed to find something that humans can do better and faster than computers.

- ~~Search through information~~
- ~~Answer complex mathematical equations~~

- ~~Play chess~~
- Recognise images

Computers weren't very good at knowing what was in a picture: all they saw was a bunch of pixels. But humans could look at a cat and see a cat. And look at a dog, and know it's not a cat.

Humans can also look at a picture of a word and read that word, even if it's twisted or stretched. Computers aren't so clever yet.

Luis' idea was simple: what if every time you wanted to open a new email account, you needed to type in some twisted letters from a picture?

CAPTCHAing humans

Luis called his new test a CAPTCHA: Completely Automated Public Turing* Test to Tell Computers and Humans Apart.

Pretty soon, CAPTCHAs were being used by millions of people to prove they were human. Even better, the spammer's computer programs could no longer open email accounts.

***Turing tests are named after Alan Turing. Alan was a computer whiz-kid and early robotics fan. He helped crack the Nazi codes during World War II. He also dreamed up the concept of digital computing. And he invented the Turing test, which works like this: You chat with two different 'people': one a computer, one a human. If you can't tell the difference between the human and the computer, then the computer is perhaps as intelligent as the human ...**

Turing at age sixteen.

Free labour

Each CAPTCHA test took less than ten seconds, but soon hundreds of millions of people were doing a test every day ...

Luis did the maths:

100,000,000 people every day

× 10 seconds

= almost 280,000 human hours every day!!! And all for free!

Luis started thinking: what if that time could be put to good use?

CAPTCHA <-> ReCAPTCHA

This was Luis' thinking:

1. There are thousands of printed books and articles that have never been typed into a computer.
2. There are thousands of people typing CAPTCHAs into their computer every day.

What if we combined the two?

Luis called his invention ReCAPTCHA, and it works like this: Instead of typing some scrambled letters to prove you're a human and stop the spam, you have to type two words:

- One is a word the computer knows. Typing this word proves you're human.

- The other is a word the computer can't read, from a printed book or article it's trying to digitise. Typing this word helps the computer learn to read, which helps it digitise faster.

Because each word is tested multiple times—and so is typed in by multiple people—the computer soon works out the correct answer.

And those pesky spammers are still blocked.

'All my projects try to accomplish public good, and in all cases we do not hide the real motive of the system—reCAPTCHA's slogan, for example, is "Stop Spam, Read Books".' Luis von Ahn

Ka-ching!

Google bought reCAPTCHA in 2009 for a big fat, unknown price (hint from Luis: between US$10 and $100 million).

You'll see reCAPTCHA on more than 100,000 websites, where millions of people type out millions of words every day.

'To date, over 750 million unique people—more than 10 per cent of humanity—have helped transcribe at least one word through reCAPTCHA.' Luis von Ahn

That's genius!

In 2006, Luis won a MacArthur Fellowship: $500,000 to work on whatever he liked. The fellowship is nicknamed a 'genius' grant.

'It's always the same joke: "Haha, I thought you were a genius." So you really can't do anything stupid anymore. But I do stupid stuff all the time.'
Luis von Ahn

Read my mind ...

Another killer idea was the ESP game, which Luis invented in 2004. Here's how it works:

You have 150 seconds to label fifteen images. You don't know who your game partner is, but they're out there, somewhere in cyberspace, labelling the same images at the same time. Your instructions are simple: Type whatever the other guy is typing.

If you both type the same label, you win fifty points. And your time starts ... now!

Around 200,000 people regularly played the ESP game for hours every week. They loved it! And they were also helping to label the millions of unlabelled images on the web.

Two birds, one stone

Another fab Luis idea: what if you could learn a new language by translating web pages?

Here are the facts:

1. Most of the web pages in the world are in English. But it costs money to translate languages.
2. Millions of people don't speak English. But it costs money to learn languages.

So Luis pulled a two-birds-one-stone and came up with a free language-learning app where students learn by translating,

> **'enabling a wealth of language-shackled information to be liberated for all of humanity.'**
> **Luis von Ahn**

How it works:

- Companies pay money to get their stuff translated.
- That money pays to host the app.
- The students use the app for free, learning and translating as they go.
- The quality of translated websites is super, because students check and double-check, all as part of their language-learning experience.

> **'Trying to translate the whole Web into every major language is a really super-crazy, ambitious thing. It's proceeding well. We're pretty confident we're going to be able to do it.' Luis von Ahn**

Do you Duolingo?

According to Luis:

By their twenty-first birthday, the average American has played 10,000 hours of video games, the equivalent

of around five years in a full-time job.
- If 100,000 people play Duolingo for just over a month, the entire contents of Wikipedia could be translated into Spanish.
- If you spend thirty-four hours playing on Duolingo, you'll get the same results as if you do a uni course for one semester.

Ideas, ideas, ideas

Luis and his team are always dreaming up new games. He says most of them are 'totally dumb'.

'I have multiple ideas per day. The vast majority of these are completely idiotic.' Luis von Ahn

But every now and then, there's something great ...

Matchin'

- **The game: You and your unknown partner see the same two pictures and have only seconds to choose which is more 'attractive'. The catch? You only earn points if you agree.**
- **The purpose: Gathers a database of information about what humans think is beautiful.**

Babble

- **The game: You and your unknown (English-speaking) partner try to agree on the best translation of a sentence. The catch? It's written in a language neither of you speak.**

- The purpose: Develops natural-sounding sentences for translations.

InTune

- The game: You and your unknown partner listen to the same audio, then race to describe it using the same labels.
- The purpose: Improves searchability of audio files by tagging them with descriptions.

Squigl

- The game: You and your unknown partner race to identify and circle an object in the same picture.
- The purpose: Labels objects within images.

Into the future

What will be the next big human computing game? Luis and his team are still working on it.

'What can you do when you can get 100 million people working on the same thing? I think we can do amazing things.' Luis von Ahn

'We're still not thinking big enough. If we have that many people all doing some little part, we could do something insanely huge for humanity.' Luis von Ahn

What would you do?

- Can you think of a great idea for a game that a) people might want to play and b) might help solve a big problem?
- Luis says learning a language with Duolingo is as effective as studying a language at university. Do you think you can learn better in a classroom or by using an app? Write a list of the pros and cons of online education versus face-to-face learning.
- Google licensed Luis' ESP game in 2006, calling it the Google Image Labeler. These days, many innovators create new technologies with the sole aim of attracting Google's attention (and dollars). What do you think of this approach?

2004 on: Thefacebook, pizza and poking

Social networking used to mean meeting for coffee or phoning a friend. Now it's texting, friending, tweeting and snapchatting. The internet has enabled people to connect in an entirely new way, launching a brand-new phenomenon: social media.

Virtually everyone on the internet follows or owns social media accounts. Billions of us are creating (and viewing) mega-loads of videos, selfies, blog posts, filtered photos and more.

So where did it all begin? Perhaps in a dental surgery.

The tech: Facebook
Invented by: Mark Zuckerberg

Meet MEZ

Say hi to Mark Zuckerberg, middle name Elliot. Mark's dad was a dentist (nickname: Dr Z) and Mum was a psychologist (nickname: Mum). Mark had three sisters and a passion for *Star Wars*.

In primary school, Mark loved reading, and even more than reading, he loved making computers do stuff. He loved it so much, his family hired him a coding tutor to help him learn faster.

But faster wasn't fast enough for Mark. He began studying university-level computing in his spare time.

Then he changed schools and met Adam D'Angelo, another computer-crazy kid. Adam inspired Mark to keep coding cool stuff*.

*A few years later, Adam became Facebook's Chief Technology Officer. A few more years after that, Adam launched the online Q&A site Quora.

My inventions, by Mark, born 14 May 1984

- ZuckNet (aged twelve-ish, with my dad): Lets you communicate with people in other rooms. Result? Dad's dental surgery is using it to let him know when patients arrive. (Me and my sisters use it too, to chat between our bedrooms.)
- Synapse (at high school, with my pal Adam): Remembers your musical taste so it can play more of what you like. Result? Microsoft want to buy it!!! I said no. So now they want to give me a job. Are you kidding? I'm still at school! I said no again.
- Course Match (aged eighteen): Helps you choose what you want to study by letting you see what other

(cool, cute and funny) students are studying. Result? Hundreds of kids are using it. And I got to study with all my besties. Yes!

- Facemash (aged nineteen): Lets you vote on whose photo is hotter, to help identify the hottest person at university. Result? So popular it started crashing my computer. Whoops. Also, I might get expelled! Whoops again.
- Harvard Connection (aged nineteen, but it's not actually my project, I'm just doing it for the cash*): Lets you link with, learn about, and arrange parties with other students from Harvard Uni. Result? ... Well. Actually. I'm going to stop working on this. Because right now, I've got a much bigger, better idea ...
- Thefacebook (aged nineteen, but I asked a bunch of friends to help): Lets you link with, learn about, and arrange parties with your friends. Result? Woah. Like, super-popular and stuff. Update: Turns out I'm a billionaire.

*Mark was hired to work on the project by some other Harvard students. When he stopped working on Harvard Connection and instead released Thefacebook, these other students were Mighty Annoyed. So they sued Mark, saying he stole their idea. Eventually, Facebook paid them $20 million cash, plus 1.2 million Facebook shares, worth plenty more millions.

What's in a name?

Back in the old days, Mark's university printed a list of every new student's name and photo. These directories were called 'facebooks'.

Mark wanted his online facebook to be the one, the only, the best. Plus, the internet domain name facebook.com was already taken. So he bought thefacebook.com instead.

After about a year, Thefacebook was going so well, Mark could afford to buy the domain name he really wanted: facebook.com. He paid $200,000, and the rest is history.

(Don't) show me the money

'I remember really vividly, you know, having pizza with my friends a day or two after I opened up the first version of Facebook at my school ... At the time I thought, "You know, someone needs to build a service like this for the world."' Mark Zuckerberg

Mark was offered $10 million for Thefacebook when it was just four months old. He said no.

Facebook grew bigger, and bigger, and attracted interest from even biggerer companies, like Microsoft and Google. They tried to buy Facebook—again and again—but Mark wouldn't sell*.

***But never give up, right? In 2007, Mark finally said yes. He sold just 1.6% of Facebook to Microsoft, for a massive $240 million.**

To poke or not to poke

Wait, what was the question?

A super-popular early Facebook function was the 'poke'. You could interact with another user just by giving them a 'poke'. But what was a poke, exactly? Well, even Mark didn't know.

'We thought it would be fun to make a feature that has no specific purpose ... So mess around with it, because you're not getting an explanation from us.'
Mark Zuckerberg

House rule: No swords

When Facebook grew too big for his university dorm, Mark moved it—and six of his buddies, including Adam—to a four-bedroom house in Silicon Valley. Here they watched movies, played X-box, threw pool parties ... and worked on Facebook.

At school, Mark had been captain of the fencing team. In the new house, he'd often grab a sword and do some fencing to help him work through a sticky problem. Eventually, his pals had to ban fencing from the house.

How many!?

The team kept checking how many users Facebook had attracted:

- After one month: 10,000
- 2004: 1 million (all from a select group of universities)
- 2005: 5.5 million (because hey, we should encourage all students to join)
- 2010: 500+ million (because we invited everyone)
- 2017: 2 billion users, every month (WTZuck? Is that a typo? Um. Nope. There really are 2 billion people using Facebook, every month—that's 2,000,000,000, in case you weren't sure).

Into the future

Mark's shares in Facebook make him a billionaire, but his salary as CEO of Facebook is just $1 a year.

Mark and his wife, Priscilla Chan, have promised to donate 99 per cent of their wealth.

'Our society has an obligation to invest now to improve the lives of all those coming into this world, not just those already here ... We will give 99 per cent of our Facebook shares—currently about $45 billion—during our lives to advance this mission.' Mark Zuckerberg and Priscilla Chan in a letter to their baby daughter, Max

What would you do?

- Facebook wasn't the first social media site, and it certainly isn't the last. There's MySpace for sharing music, Flickr for sharing photos, LinkedIn for sharing job opportunities. Some sites die off, others stay mega-popular, and new sites are always popping up. Who would've dreamed that disappearing photos would be so popular? Or 140-character blog posts? Or DIY photo filters? What's your idea for a cracker social media site?
- Imagine you're applying for your dream job. You do well at the interview. Your new team seems great. Then your potential boss asks to see your social media profiles. Yikes. What do your social media accounts say about you? Would you show them to your parents? Your besties? What about your boss?

2005 on: Wind-up batteries, sunlit screens and One Laptop Per Child

More than one billion people live without mobile phone coverage or internet access. But what would happen if every child in the world could access the internet, and all the information, inspiration and cat-video-distraction that goes with it? A holography student named Mary Lou decided to find out.

The tech: A super-cheap wind-up laptop, called XO, made by One Laptop Per Child
Developed by: Mary Lou Jepsen

Look into my screen

Screens. You spend hours staring into them. They're like a gateway to another world. And right from the start, Mary Lou Jepsen was an expert at making awesome screens. She started by making holograms when she was at school, then she co-founded her own company, called MicroDisplay, where she focused on making screens smaller and smaller and smaller. She even worked with Intel as Chief Technology Officer of their display division.

Then she woke up one day and decided it was time for something else. A new adventure.

Sweet screen smarts

In January 2005, Mary Lou joined One Laptop Per Child as its only employee. The idea was to empower the world's poorest children to create, share and learn together by … well. Hopefully you can work that bit out by yourself.

Mary Lou's job was to design the perfect laptop for the job:

- so cheap, you could give one to every child
- so sturdy, it could survive sweaty monsoonal storms, biting desert heat and being dropped by your little brother about a million times
- so technically clever it needed hardly any power to run.

'... a solar cell is all that is needed to power a calculator. Wouldn't it be great if we could do the same for cell phones, laptops, tablets and personal medical devices?' **Mary Lou Jepsen**

The new 'new'

Mary Lou used her sweet screen smarts to create a prototype laptop, and she totally smashed it. (As in, she did a great job. She didn't smash the laptop—she'd made it smash-resistant.)

She worked on:

- new screen technology—so you can read your screen even if you're outside in bright sunshine
- new battery technology—so you can use your laptop for longer
- new power technology—so if your village doesn't have electricity, you can solar power your laptop, or crank it up with a hand-powered crank
- new networking technology—so you don't need expensive underground cables to access the internet
- new kid-friendly software and user interface—so you can teach yourself how to use your laptop to write music, make videos, work on projects with your friends ... and more.

'The architecture we've created is very powerful, not just for low-cost laptops, but for high-end laptops as well.' **Mary Lou Jepsen**

Being green

Mary Lou's laptop was named XO, but it was also called 'the greenest laptop on the planet' because of its super-efficient energy use and repairability.

'Our machines are half the size and weight of a typical laptop, and our laptops are repairable by children and by locals. You can change out plastic parts quite easily, including the screens. Five-year-olds can change the screen on our laptop because it's actually that easy.' Mary Lou Jepsen

$100 laptop

Less than a year after she started work, Mary-Lou unveiled her prototype laptop. It had no moving parts, no hard drive, and heaps of fans (as in enthusiastic supporters, not air blowers).

One Laptop Per Child was hoping to sell the laptops for just $100. They ended up costing closer to $200. At the time, other laptops were selling for nearly ten times that price.

Governments in more than fifty countries and across twenty-five languages have bought more than a billion dollars' worth of Mary Lou's laptops.

'Children will be able to learn by doing, not just through instruction or rote memorisation. And they will be able to open a new front in their education: peer-to-peer learning.' Kofi Annan, former United Nations Secretary-General

'They came to be used for all the day's work. With a computer, we could find out about many things that we didn't know existed in Uruguay.' Seventeen-year-old Micaela Rodriguez, who received an XO laptop when she was seven

'I think there's new life in the schools we've gone into … It has to be the most powerful thing we can do with computers.' Mary Lou Jepsen

(Parachuting) into the future

One Laptop Per Child still exists, but Mary Lou has moved on. She's worked for Facebook's Oculus VR project, and for Google X on super-high-tech projects, like the driverless car.

By inventing XO, Mary Lou changed the face of computing. But did giving kids a laptop each really help their education? That depends on who you ask.

Some researchers found that having a laptop didn't improve kids' scores on maths and reading tests. Others found that having a laptop helps kids learn how to learn.

Some people say developing countries should spend their money on water and food, not laptops. Others say education and knowledge is the pathway to development and success.

And some people say One Laptop Per Child should provide more training for teachers on how to use and look after laptops in their classrooms. Others say kids are so curious and clever, they can learn how to use a laptop, even if one was just parachuted down into the middle of a remote village.

'Think about these machines going into refugee camps. If you end up in a refugee camp, you have been through hell. It would be a really good thing if you could lose yourself in a laptop and start to find another world.' Mary Lou Jepsen

What would you do?

- What do you think about the One Laptop Per Child project? Does failing to provide 'one laptop per child' make it a failure? Is it too soon to judge whether it is a success? What successes have been achieved along the way?
- Mary Lou recently launched a company called Openwater, which aims to make medical imaging of your brain super-cheap. How could you use this technology? What if you could literally take pictures of thoughts? What sort of device would you create?

2010 on: Blog posts, 4 am starts and Fiftysix Creations

Soon, where laptops walked, tablets and smartphones began to run entire marathons. Using a pocket-sized sliver of technology, you can pretty much access anything on the web, anytime, anyplace. Gone are the keyboards and the mouses (mice?)—now you just slide your finger across the screen. And gone are the fights about whether to turn left or right and who's in charge of the map anyway. Siri-ously.

You can consume the world's media with the swipe of a screen. But what if you could create the world, not just consume it?

The tech: A DIY computer tablet that you can build and program
Invented by: Taj Pabari, 2017 Queensland Young Australian of the Year

In the money

Taj Pabari didn't really love school. Instead of playing by the rules, he just wanted to play. He was suspended several times, and nearly expelled.

But that didn't stop him from making the most of his time. When he was eleven, he started a blog, posting reviews of new games and technologies. The reviews were written by kids, for kids. As the blog grew more popular, Taj started making money from advertisements that companies paid to put on his site.

He used this money to pay other kids to write more reviews, which led to more traffic on his site, and so his business grew.

'By the end of primary school, I was earning $10 a day from advertisements, which I thought was pretty cool.' Taj Pabari

Fiftysix Creations

Taj started his next company when he was fourteen. The idea grew from an assignment: kids had to use the school's 3D printer to stick two bits of plastic together. Pretty simple instructions. But Taj wondered if you could instead use the printer to make a plastic shell for a mini-computer. Turned out you could.

He started a company, calling it MechTech Creations (later Fiftysix Creations). His idea was to invent a computer tablet that kids could build and then use to create their own apps and blogs, and ultimately start their own businesses. He recruited a couple of mates and crowdfunded the cash to get started.

Then he began getting up at 4 am each day so he could put in three hours work on the project before starting school.

Fiftysix mistakes

Taj loved to watch YouTube videos of Bill Gates, Steve Jobs and Mark Zuckerberg making speeches. He learned that success comes with hard work, the ability to think outside the box, and the opportunity to fail.

'Embrace failure. Learn from your mistakes, and perhaps don't make the same mistakes over and over again.' Taj Pabari

Do you have an idea? Start young

Taj thinks your school years are the perfect time to start making your dreams a reality. He says school isn't about absorbing knowledge, but learning how to create it.

'School's only from eight to three pm. You have so much free time to start a business, or start a social change movement. If you're passionate about something, take the action, and the magic will happen. Just start!' Taj Pabari

Into the future

Taj wants to take his tablets beyond Australia to help kids in poorer countries too. He's already donated tablets to kids in Nepal, India and Africa.

By 2020, he aims to teach a million children about science, creativity and entrepreneurship.

What would you do?

- How much spare time do you have before and after school? Can you think of something creative you'd like to spend that time on? What about something that might change the world?
- When Taj started his company, he was too young to be its official director. He had to employ an adult to run his company. How would you feel about giving someone else control of your dream?

2010 on: Smartphones, myKicks and Fruit Ninjas

What do people do on their devices all day? Let your imagination run wild, dream up almost anything, and there's probably a phone app that does it. There's an app for making fart noises, and one that lets you pop virtual bubble wrap. There's an app on how to survive an apocalypse, and another to practise counting a million dollars. There's one that fakes important phone calls (like from your doctor, or your fashion designer), and another that lets you send fake messages to yourself from whoever you want ('I got u a backstage pass so see u after the show <3').

But just because there are apps for almost anything, doesn't mean there are apps for everything. As technology develops, the possibilities for apps are shooting for the stars ... and for a goal.

The tech: myKicks: an app that shows the world how awesome your soccer kicks are
Invented by: Holly Ade-Simpson

Sporting chance

Holly Ade-Simpson loved sports. At school she was captain of the netball and volleyball teams. She also loved science. She was planning to study physics at uni when she was sidetracked into electronics and computer engineering. The only problem? She'd never really worked with computers.

'My very first day of university they made me put together a computer hard drive, and I freaked out. It was super difficult.' Holly Ade-Simpson

But Holly learned fast, and found she loved the ups and downs of technology.

'You can have a great day of coding and everything works, and the next day nothing works. You need to keep pushing. To keep fighting.' Holly Ade-Simpson

One, two, ~~three~~

One day Holly applied for an internship at Google. After two epic phone interviews and two technical interviews, she was in.

'You have to have something called Googliness to get an internship at Google. It's a way of life, you're supporting other people, you're wanting everyone else to do well.' Holly Ade-Simpson

'They watched me code, which was quite nerve-wracking, but it was fun.' Holly Ade-Simpson

Holly rocked Google and was invited back for another internship. She jumped at the opportunity.

But when Google asked Holly back a third time, she said no. They mentioned it would be in AI research, which she loved. She still said no.

Because Holly had another idea brewing ... and it had the potential to go global.

'At Google there are so many incredible minds with differing passions, however in my own company I can influence all areas to focus on my passion of integrating technology into our everyday lives for the better.' Holly Ade-Simpson

Get your myKicks

Soccer is the world's most popular sport, with over a billion players. So what if you could encourage even of a fraction of them to buy your app?

That's the thinking behind Holly's app, myKicks. It's a super-powerful tool for recording and analysing your mad soccer skills. You don't need a special ball or expensive hardware, just your smartphone.

Using artificial intelligence and augmented reality, the app can:

- track your kicks
- provide stats on your speed and accuracy
- calculate the possibility that you'd have scored against a goalkeeper.

You can also post your best kicks on social media. And your worst kicks too, if you really want to.

Teamwork on-field and off

Holly is now the Chief Technology Officer at her start-up company, Formalytics, leading a team of developers.

'We're all really driven to make sure this is successful. We all trust each other to do our jobs, and we all cherish each other's input.'
Holly Ade-Simpson

Into the future

The myKicks technology tracks the shape of the ball. Theoretically, it can be adjusted to work with any round ball: tennis, cricket, hockey, ping-pong ...

The hardest thing, Holly says, is working out what direction to take the company in next.

What would you do?

- Several Aussie app developers have hit the big time. For example, Shainiel Deo made millions with the invention of Fruit Ninja. Brainstorm ideas for an app that you could create.
- Would you turn down an internship at Google? What if you had a really awesome idea?

PART FIVE
WRESTLING

Botnets, spam and zombie computers

Steal your secrets, crash your website, empty your bank account, delete your hard drive, or simply prove a point. Computer criminals spend their careers working on clever ways to take over your computer and ruin your day.

The tech: An ordinary computer or smartphone (maybe even yours), gone bad
Controlled by: Nobody knows. Mwa ha ha ha!

Q: How do you know if your PC is a zombie?

A: You don't*.

A zombie computer looks like an ordinary computer. It behaves like an ordinary computer. But its electronic brain is possessed by criminals and its memory is infected with malicious code, called malware (rhymes with underwear).

***If you notice that your computer runs a little slow, it may be doing zombie work in the background.**

Spammity spam! Wonderful spam!

Before spam was junk email, it was a type of canned meat. The word 'spam' came to mean 'unwanted and unasked for' because of comedy TV series *Monty Python's Flying Circus*.

In one historic (and hysterical) skit, a waitress lists a café menu, which is mostly spam, but her voice is drowned out by other café customers (who happen to be Vikings, because why not?) singing a song whose lyrics are also mostly spam, thus spamming the conversation. Spam.

Epidemic

Billions of spam emails are sent every day, and most are sent by the world's 100,000,000+ zombie computers.

Any computer connected to the internet can be targeted by criminals. Once your computer has been infected with a malicious virus or bot (short for robot, not bottom), attackers can use it for whatever they like. And you won't even know.

Trojan horses

One morning, you open your front door. On your doorstep is an enormous and rather pretty wooden horse. Do you:

a) invite the horse in for cake.
b) tip the horse upside-down, give it a good shake, and discover dozens of bad guys hidden inside.

In the original story, the Trojan horse tricked the people of Troy into letting enemy soldiers into their city. It was literally a horse, an enormous wooden sculpture left just outside Troy's locked gates. The people of Troy assumed the horse was a gift. They opened the gates and wheeled it in. But the horse was hollow, and full of warriors and spies. When the people let the horse in, they unwittingly let their enemy in, too. And alas, their city was lost.

In computing, Trojan horses work in the same way: they trick you.

Download me to proteckt your compewta
Clik here to view a message from your bank
A friend send you this HILARIOUS video! Watch now!

You might be tricked into visiting an infected website or downloading an infected file. Either way, the enemy has found a way inside your computer.

Off with its head

Bots that are linked into a network of zombie computers are called botnets. One botnet, named Rustock, coordinated around a million zombie slaves. Rustock ran from 2006–2011, and at its peak could send 30 billion spam emails a day. That's 1.25 billion emails an hour. More than 20 million emails a minute. Or almost 350,000 emails a second. Which is somewhat faster than you can type.

To take Rustock down, police simultaneously stormed nine command centres in multiple countries. They successfully beheaded the botnet, and global spam dropped by 30 per cent overnight.

But no worries. New botnets soon sprang up to take Rustock's place. And who was the evil mastermind behind Rustock? We still don't know.

Zombie hordes, attack!

Botnets can also cripple a website in what's called a 'denial of service' attack. Anti-spam sites, like SPEWS (the Spam Prevention Early Warning System), are often targeted in these attacks.

Imagine 100,000 zombie computers all heading to the SPEWS website at the same time.

Most websites aren't built for that kind of attention. As the zombies flood in, the site crashes. The zombies can't use it. And any legit non-zombie users can't use it either. Which is the aim of the attack. Service: denied.

Mafiaboy to white hat hacker

In 2000, fifteen-year-old Michael Calce—alias Mafiaboy—enslaved the computer networks of several universities using his bedroom computer. Showing off to his friends, he used the universities' computers to crash websites including Amazon, CNN, Dell, E*Trade, eBay and Yahoo! (which back then was the world's biggest search engine).

'Before that moment, I was just an ordinary kid, growing up in the suburbs.' Michael Calce

The FBI hunted Michael down and arrested him. After that, Michael decided to use his powers for good, not evil. He worked as a white hat hacker: someone who helps companies find and fix their computer security problems.

'Ever since I first laid hands on a PC, at six years old, I knew my life would be forever linked to computers.' Michael Calce

Into the future

Zombification takes only minutes. To protect your computer, set your security software to auto-update.

Anti-virus: Automatically update
Anti-spyware: Automatically update
Updates: Install automatically

Sadly, even the best-defended computer can't protect you from yourself.

- Don't give your personal details out on the web.
- Don't click on unknown links.
- And don't download from dodgy sites, dodgy thumb drives, or from your friend's dodgy zombie computer.

What would you do?

- Many hackers end up working in computer security. Would you employ a hacker to manage your computer security? Why? Why not?
- Sometimes malware works not by crashing your computer, but by holding it hostage. Called ransomware, this type of program encrypts all your data, and won't give it back unless you pay a fee. What would you do if this happened to you? How can you avoid being the victim of ransomware?
- Often, spam email tries to trick you into thinking you've won the lottery, inherited millions, or are being offered a fantastic job. Try writing your own spam email. How could you entice your victims to click on a malware link?

Rock climbing, gingerbread houses and a Security Princess

Professional hackers attack computer networks around the world a squillion times a day. Some work for good, others for evil.

The tech: The cyber safety of Google's internet browser, Chrome
Managed by: Parisa Tabriz

Hack or be hacked

Parisa Tabriz's mum was a nurse and her dad was a doctor. As a kid, she was into art, sport, and putting up with her two squirmy brothers. But then she started engineering at uni, and she discovered computing.

Parisa began building a website using a service called Angelfire. The service was free, but only if you included their ads. Parisa didn't want to include their ads on her site, so she developed a hack to remove them.

Angelfire found out, and fixed the hole. So Parisa discovered a new hack to remove the ads. It went on like this for quite a while.

'I liked the challenge of that. That's how I got into computer security.' Parisa Tabriz

Hack

/hæk/ *verb*

1. To gain unauthorised access to a computer system
2. To create a new and clever solution
3. To chop with repeated, ruthless blows

noun

informal: an act of computer hacking

Black hat, white hat

White hat hackers use their skills for good, not evil. They often earn their money by helping to find and fix security issues.

Black hat hackers are the opposite: they steal and sell the information they find. They're also called crackers, because they break into things like secure computer systems or protected software.

Grey hat hackers are a bit of both ... After all, who gets to decide what is good and what is evil?

You've been pwned (rhymes with 'owned')

One day, Parisa's website was hacked by someone else. She got mad ... then she got even. She joined SIGMil, a student club focused on internet security. She researched wireless networking security and technologies for protecting privacy. She spent a summer interning at Google. And then she started fighting fire with fire.

Security Princess

Parisa's job at Google was Information Security Engineer, which she decided was way too boring. She changed her business cards so her job title was Security Princess. When she was promoted to head of Google Chrome's security team, she changed her job title to Browser Boss.

'Hacking information security is fun, and I'm pretty lucky I get paid to work on it with the world's best.' Parisa Tabriz

Parisa now leads a team of security experts and hacker engineers in the never-ending quest to keep Google Chrome safe from malicious hackers*. Her job is to find (and fix) ways to hack into Chrome before the black hats find them.

*She's also worked on software security for the US Government and the White House.

Stuff I like, by Parisa

- Google
- Gelato making
- Glass burning
- Gingerbread-house making*
- GRock climbing

*Parisa's family has a holiday tradition of designing and building gingerbread houses. Her houses include the White House, a Pacman game, a laptop and a cryptography house, decorated with 0s and 1s.

WANTED: Bugs REWARD: $100,000

Ever heard of Gzob Qq? Gzob is the online name of an anonymous hacker who collected $100,000 from Google's Security Reward Program in 2016 and 2017. Google's deal is,

if you can find a bug in their software and report it to them, you'll receive a chunky payout.

Since the program started in 2010, Google has paid more than $9 million in rewards.

Probably a small thing …

In 2017 Ezequiel Pereira, a high-school student from Uruguay, won $10,000 when he discovered a bug in Google's App Engine.

'On July 11th, I was bored, so I tried to find some bug at Google.' Ezequiel Pereira

After many failed attempts, Ezequiel found his way into a confidential Google page. He reported the bug immediately.

'I thought to myself, "Cool, this is probably a small thing that isn't worth a dime" … Some weeks later I got an email right after getting out of school that said my report was worth much more than a dime.' Ezequiel Pereira

My other computer … is your computer

Hackers spend a lot of time finding security bugs they can use to make your computer their own.

Part of Parisa's job is teaching coders how to find and fix bugs in their code before it is released.

'Unfortunately, no-one, including me, is unhackable. That's sobering, but for better or worse, it parallels the safety of the real world.' Parisa Tabriz

Hats off to hackers

Computer hackers are usually self-taught, resourceful, highly creative and driven by a challenge. They're expert at adapting and personalising computer systems, at discovering technology limitations and possibilities, and at making computers perform in new ways.

None of these things is against the law.

'A lot of the people we hire just have this curiosity to try to understand something. And maybe a bit of a mischievous slant, to try to do something unexpected.' Parisa Tabriz

Rats!

The world's first hacker may well have been the magician Nevil Maskelyne.

In 1903, London's scientific elite had gathered for a public demonstration of a new technology: supposedly 'secure' wireless telegraphy.

Everyone was waiting to receive a 'confidential' Morse-coded message from the technology's Italian inventor, Guglielmo

Marconi, who was 300 miles away. Suddenly, an unexpected message from Nevil appeared:

Rats! Rats! Rats!
There was a young fellow of Italy,
who diddled the public quite prettily.

Nevil wasn't a great poet, but it was a great hack, revealing security flaws in the 'secure' technology.

'Can you do me a favour?'

Once the FBI's most wanted hacker, Kevin Mitnick began his criminal career at thirteen, when he sweet-talked a bus driver into helping him with a 'school project'. Kevin's 'project' was to buy his own card punch, giving him free travel on all of Los Angeles' buses.

Kevin went on to hack dozens of companies, but he didn't hack for money. He worked for the fun of it. Along the way he learned loads of IT and coding skills, but his most valuable skill was social engineering. He was charming and friendly. He was helpful and funny. He pretended to be whoever you would most trust. Then he took you—and your trust—for a ride.

'It's not that people are stupid. We are just human beings, and our trust can be exploited.' Kevin Mitnick

After spending five years in jail, Kevin began a new life as a white hat hacker.

Poetry and beauty

Like Ada Lovelace, hacker Anna Moore sees poetry in computing. Unlike Ada, Anna's parents encouraged her into hacking. They bought her a computer, let her play with it as much as she liked, and drove her to hack meetings. She was encouraged to set her own limits, and deal with the consequences. Aged just fifteen, she won the CyberEthical Surfivor competition at DefCon, the annual hacker conference.

'Hacking is an art of poetry and beauty.' Anna Moore

Script kiddies and vandals

While it takes smarts to write a computer program, even fools can run one. Wannabe hackers who use automated hacking tools for pranks and online graffiti are called 'script kiddies'.

Into the future

Many of history's hackers have gone on to change the world.

- Tim Berners-Lee, caught hacking while at Oxford University, went on to invent the World Wide Web.
- Kevin Mitnick now runs a respected IT security company.
- Julian Assange* went on to found WikiLeaks.

- Steve Wozniak and Steve Jobs created Apple Computers.

And a new generation of hackers are also contributing:

- Jan Koum invented WhatsApp.
- Drew Houston created Dropbox.
- George Hotz, the teenager who hacked the PlayStation 3 and the iPhone, has invented, among other things, a '$1000 box' that can convert ordinary cars into driverless vehicles. George has also collected $150,000 in bug bounties from Google's Security Reward Program.

***Never heard of Julian? Read the next chapter.**

What would you do?

- **Say you had the power to access any computer system in the world. Which system would you choose? What would you do with the information or data you uncovered?**
- **Some people believe we should run Hacker High Schools, teaching new hackers the skills and knowledge they need to hack responsibly. What do you think of this idea?**
- **Ordinary people are encouraged to help Parisa and her team, thanks to Google's Security Reward Programs. In 2017, Google announced their Google Play Security Reward Program, which pays hackers who find bugs in popular apps. Other companies also pay bug bounties to people who find and report bugs. So what are you waiting for?**

Classified secrets, leaks and democracy

It doesn't matter whether you're a good guy, a bad guy, or something in between. Thanks to the internet, it's really hard to keep a secret.

What you do, say or write can be recorded (or hacked), and then published for the world to see. All you need is somewhere to publish it.

The tech: **WikiLeaks: a website for spreading secrets**
Controlled by: **Julian Assange**

37 schools in 50 towns

Julian Assange's mum and dad were both anti-war protesters. When he was little, his mum and step-dad owned a travelling theatre, so he moved a lot. Later, to escape a nasty relationship, he and his mum lived on the run for years.

By the time he was fourteen, Julian says he'd gone to thirty-seven schools and lived in fifty towns. One of those moves was to a house opposite an electronics shop.

Julian spent some time checking the shop out, and he liked what he saw. He began teaching himself how to code.

The International Subversives

Julian started seriously hacking when he was sixteen. He worked from his Melbourne bedroom, using the codename Mendax.

Mendax
From the Latin *splendide mendax*: 'nobly false', or 'untruthful for a good reason'

He and two friends started a hacking group, calling it the International Subversives. The three of them produced their own top-secret magazine, packed with tips on how to hack and phreak phone lines. It was a super-exclusive publication: they were the only three readers.

Julian began hacking into mega-secure networks, like

NASA, the US Defense Agency and the Pentagon. He could have copied the sensitive information he saw and sold it for millions, but he didn't. He hacked purely for the thrill.

Nortel nortel

Julian was finally caught when he was twenty. Police charged him with hacking into the NorTel telecommunications network, which he had indeed done.

He'd written some password-cracking software, hacked into NorTel's network, then used the software to crack thousands of NorTel passwords.

But how did he hack into their network in the first place? He correctly guessed the log-on details of a single account:

username: nortel
password: nortel

Julian faced ten years in jail, but because he hadn't acted maliciously, the judge let him off with just a fine.

Crack this

How vulnerable are your passwords? These are some of the world's most common (and worst) passwords:

- 123456
- password
- qwerty
- baseball
- monkey
- letmein

- abc123
- 111111
- superman
- shadow
- trustno1

Make maths, not war

Julian studied maths and physics at uni, but not for long. He dropped out when he realised some of the university's research was being used by the military.

He became very passionate about our right to say what we think, and our right to know what governments are doing. He started a website to help share secrets that he believed shouldn't be kept. He called it WikiLeaks: *'a giant library of the world's most persecuted documents'.*

The site lets people 'leak' information: they can upload classified and top-secret documents without anyone knowing who they are.

Julian said he wanted to fight oppression, conspiracy and corruption by revealing the truth.

'The more secretive or unjust an organisation is, the more leaks induce fear and paranoia in its leadership and planning coterie.' Julian Assange

Whistleblowers

People who 'leak' secrets are called whistleblowers. Like referees, they 'blow the whistle' when they see unfair or illegal activities.

Julian thinks the identity of whistleblowers should always be protected, regardless of the circumstances (a bit like Superman and Batman). But not everyone agrees.

US soldier Chelsea Manning leaked more than 720,000 documents revealing the way the US was fighting wars in Iraq and Afghanistan. She downloaded the docs to a rewritable CD of Lady Gaga's music, because no one would ever suspect something labelled 'Lady Gaga' could actually be important. She mentioned this little detail to a friend, and he mentioned it to someone else.

Next thing, Chelsea was arrested and charged with twenty-two offences, including 'aiding the enemy', which is punishable by death in the US. She was sentenced to thirty-five years in jail. After serving six years' jail time, she was pardoned by then-President Barack Obama.

You're leaking!

WikiLeaks has published more than 10 million classified and secret documents, including videos and emails. The leaks detail corruption and crime in countries all over the world.

Some people say the leaked information has fuelled national uprisings, or changed the way people think about war. Others say it has put people in danger, with no real public benefit.

Some people call Julian a high-tech terrorist. And they might be right:

'To topple kings someone must die. One soon revels in the carnage of change.' Julian Assange

Others want to nominate him for the Nobel Peace Prize. And they might be right, too:

'Every time we witness an injustice and do not act, we train our character to be passive in its presence and thereby eventually lose all ability to defend ourselves and those we love.' Julian Assange

And the winner is ...

During the 2016 US election, WikiLeaks released thousands of Presidential candidate Hillary Clinton's private emails. And in his election campaign, Donald Trump praised WikiLeaks several times, announcing 'I love WikiLeaks'. It turned out there was nothing illegal in Hillary's emails, but the leaks made people suspicious of her all the same.

Donald Trump won the election, a result that has changed the world. But did WikiLeaks really change the result?

Who leaked those emails, and why? And why did WikiLeaks choose to publish them at such a sensitive time? There's no proof, but there are many theories ...

'The Russians interfered with our elections in the 2016 cycle. They did it with purpose. They did it with sophistication, with overwhelming technical efforts, and it was an "active measures" campaign driven from the top of that government.' James Comey, FBI Director in 2017

Was it my non-Russian aunty's best friend's cat?

Julian says he knows who gave Hillary's private emails to WikiLeaks, and it wasn't the Russians.

But perhaps the Russians gave the emails to someone else.

Or perhaps they gave them to someone else to give to someone else to give to Julian.

Or (and this is my fave theory), perhaps they gave the emails to someone else to give to someone else to give to their friend's aunty to give to someone else to give to Julian.

Ultimately, we're talking international espionage here, so you can only imagine what really happened.

Social media vs democracy

WikiLeaks wasn't the only website that may have influenced the 2016 US election. Organisations from Russia paid Facebook, Twitter and Google to spread misleading information via the internet. Phony companies paid them to run biased ads. Fake accounts used bots to automatically share fake news, fake statistics and reports about fake events. And ordinary people like you and me read and spread the lies.

Technology has been used to sway opinions in many other countries. Some governments block websites they don't agree with, or shut down internet access at key times. Others use social media to control conversations and manipulate debates. After all, if 96 per cent of people think I'm great, you should, too.

Beginner's guide to being hacked

Imagine you have a huge secret you'd do anything to protect. Unfortunately, there are a thousand ways for hackers to uncover your secret, just by trawling through your personal data. And perhaps the easiest way for hackers to get their grubby hands on your data is for you to give it to them:

1. Hackers set up a fake public wi-fi network with a trustworthy name, like Free_Telstra or wifi-Public or Xpresso_public or I_am_not_a_hacker_pinky_promise. (Okay, maybe not that last one, but you get the idea.)
2. You log in to the fake wi-fi network.
3. Everything seems normal, but whatever you do online now goes via the hacker. Kiss goodbye to your private logins, passwords and personal details.

Into the future

For years, Julian has lived in a converted office in the UK's Ecuadorian Embassy. He is afraid that if he leaves, he'll be arrested, sent to the US and tossed in jail.

WikiLeaks continues to publish a stream of leaked information ... What will be next?

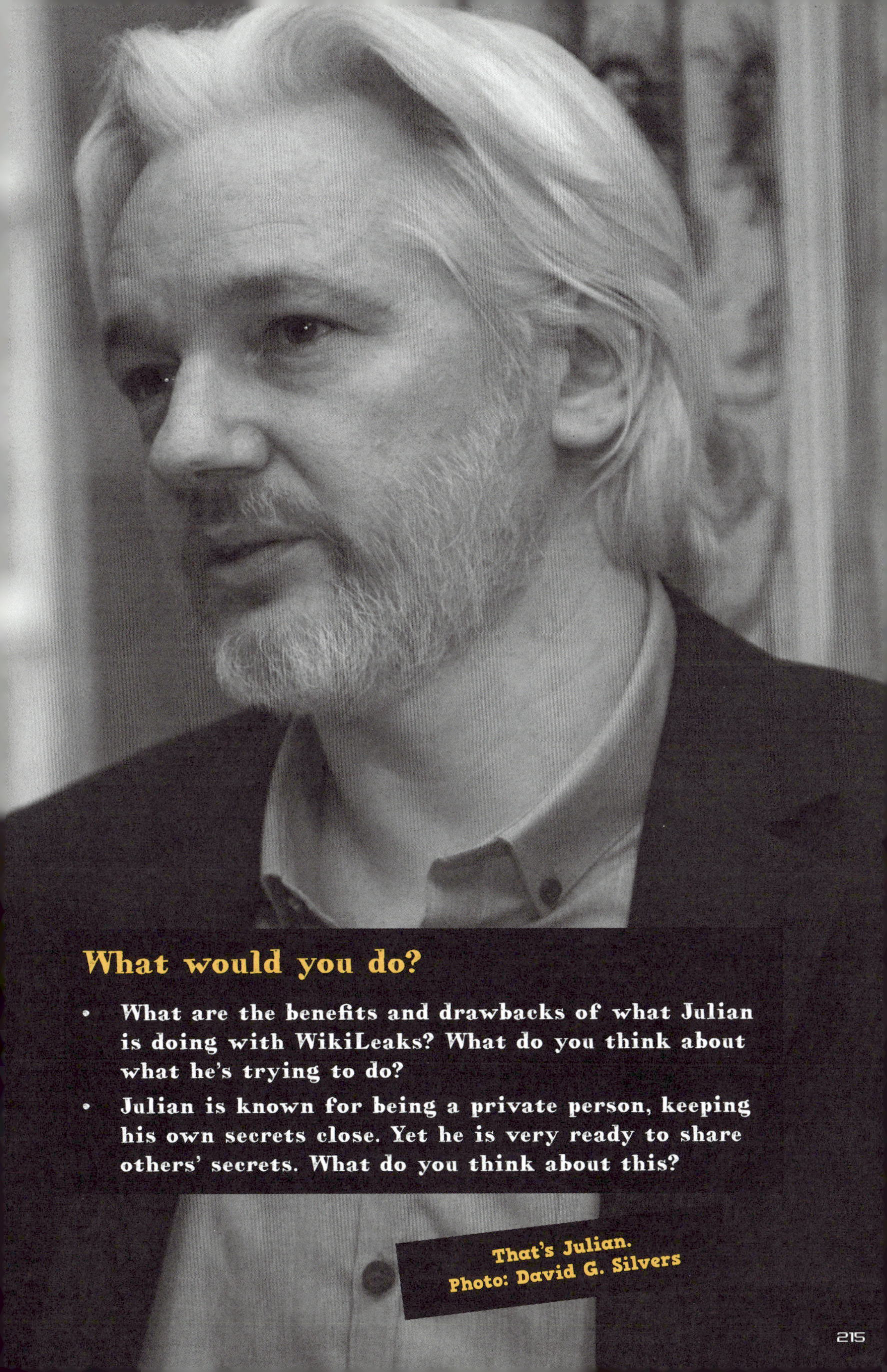

What would you do?

- What are the benefits and drawbacks of what Julian is doing with WikiLeaks? What do you think about what he's trying to do?
- Julian is known for being a private person, keeping his own secrets close. Yet he is very ready to share others' secrets. What do you think about this?

That's Julian.
Photo: David G. Silvers

Your life online, fake news and seven amazing tricks to recognise ->clickbait<

Hackers don't need to steal your data. Most of us are literally giving it away.

Computers collect data on the way that atoms smash into pieces, the way that stars explode, and the way that billions of us like to live our lives. Never before have we created and recorded so much data.

Some of this data is used for science. Some of it is used to sell you stuff. Lots of stuff.

The tech: The world's most powerful technologies
Controlled by: People who want your money

I know what you did last Friday

Everything you do can and will be used against you by advertisers.

- **Your mobile phone** lets companies know where you are, how fast you're travelling, where you go and for how long (Walks to work? Let's sell them shoes and sunscreen!)
- **Your credit card** tells companies where you shop, what you buy and when you buy it (Friday night? Let's sell them pizza and a movie!).
- **Your phone company** knows who you call and how long you chat for (Friend in Canada? Let's sell them flights and maple syrup!)
- **Your internet search engine** knows who you're interested in and what you'd like to wear to that party (No longer got the hots for Zayn Malik? Let's sell them tattoo removal!).

Computers can crunch the data that is your life, providing companies with the best information about how you like to live, when you're likely to die, and what you'd like to spend your money on.

Your life as big data

Some might say Facebook owns your life. Well, not quite. What Facebook does own is a massive database of information about the private and public lives of its billions of users. This information allows Facebook to sell targeted advertising. Do you like dogs? Do you wear hats? Do you want to travel? Here are some ads for dog food, hat shops and holidays.

And who decides which Facebook posts are appropriate? Facebook.

Who decides which photos are not okay to share? Facebook.

Facebook has the power to delete or promote your posts. Facebook can decide which of your friends see your updates, and which posts appear in your own updates. Which means that Facebook controls your newsfeed. You read what Facebook wants you to read.

Get rich quicker

Thanks to the internet, ordinary people can now access an incredible wealth of information.

But just as this technology empowers the weak, it also empowers the powerful. Because who owns the data being collected? Who has the resources to jump on new opportunities? And who can buy the best marketing campaigns?

TWO SHOCKING SECRETS REVEALED BY CELEBRITY CATERPILLAR!!!

Once upon a time, only editors, reporters, their bosses, advertisers and sponsors had the power to create the news. That meant they controlled what you read and saw.

Now anyone can publish anything. Which is great, because it means we're all empowered. But it also sucks, because it means what you publish doesn't even have to be true.

PS: Celebrity caterpillars are actually a thing.
PPS: No, they're not. I made that bit up. Did you click on it?

98 per cent of facts are fake*

Fake news is 'news' that someone made up. Sometimes it's invented to trick or manipulate you. Other times it's just about making more money by getting more eyeballs on ads.

Thanks to social media and the internet, a piece of fake news can be shared (and believed) by hundreds of thousands of people in a single day. Pro-Trump supporters shared fake news stories 30 million times in the lead-up to the 2016 US election. Pro-Clinton supporters shared fake stories more than 7.6 million times.

Trouble is, by the time you discover that a piece of news is fake, it's often too late. Your mind is made up. Many people never discover (or believe) the truth.

***This is not a fact.**

Amazing dog cuts hair for wealthy robots!!!

Dramatic hyped-up titles aren't called 'clickbait' for nothing. They work by baiting you to click on the story and visit a new web page. The more pages you visit, the more ads you'll see. And the more ads you see, the more money people who run the websites make.

Cloudy with a (calculated) chance of Lamborghinis

Computers can search data to make connections faster than any human. This means computers can predict everything from the weather to the winner of the Triple J Hottest 100.

They can also predict what car you might buy, what movies you might watch, and even who you're most likely to vote for. Coders are working on computer programs that can predict the world's breaking news before it breaks, just by studying what's happening on Twitter.

The Internet of Things

Thanks to the internet, our computers and devices can talk to each other. We've used the internet to create massive computer grids, where ordinary computers work together on huge challenges, like curing cancer or discovering life on other planets.

And because of the internet, we don't even need to store our own files—we just share them with companies who look after them for us, in the 'cloud', so we can access our stuff anywhere, any time.

But why stop at sharing computers and files? What about our cars? Our activity trackers? Our ovens, fridges and smart tattoos? Why not network everything? This vision—where all the things in our life are networked together to share information—is called The Internet of Things. Your phone can tell your aircon to switch on, because your car is on the way home. And your car can play your favourite music, check its own tyre pressure and make sure you closed the garage door.

But what will happen when everything is connected? What happens to all that data, all that information. How can we use it for the good of the planet, and not simply to sell us more stuff?

Into the future

Computers are getting smarter. Way back in 1952, UNIVAC was able to correctly predict who would win the US Presidential election. Early opinion polls picked Adlai Stevenson as the winner, but UNIVAC crunched the numbers and predicted Dwight Eisenhower would romp home. And so he did.

What will computers achieve by 2052?

What would you do?

- How much personal information should you share online? Design a poster that encourages people to think before sharing private information online.
- Do you believe in freedom of information? Should everyone be allowed access to all information? Who decides what information should be censored or private?

PUMAs, AI and the robot apocalypse

We invented calculators to help us with maths. Then we made those calculators into computers that help us navigate, communicate and create. Now we're teaching those computers to learn, so they can do things way better than us.

Um. Does this sound wise to you?

The tech: Robots and AI (artificial intelligence)

Controlled by: Robots and AI

The world's first robot? I EMVI u

Victor Scheinman wasn't always a fan of robots.

'My first contact with robots occurred when I went to see the movie *The Day the Earth Stood Still*, as a kid maybe about eight years old or maybe nine years old. And I was terrified by the robot in that movie and had nightmares over it.' Victor Scheinman

But he soon came around. When Victor was in high school, he built a voice-controlled typewriter. He called it EMVI, short for Electro Mechanical Voice Inscriber. He went on to work on heaps of stuff: hydrofoil boats, lunar gravity simulators, missile-carrying submarines, NASA's Saturn rocket engines and lunar lander ...

And in 1969, at university, Victor designed one of the world's first robots. It was a computer-controlled arm, and he designed it at Stanford University, so it's called the Stanford Arm. What an incredible name!

Victor's robotic arm went on to become the PUMA: Programmable Universal Machine for Assembly, or Programmable Universal Manipulation Arm. PUMAs have been used to perform medical operations, solve cube puzzles, and build everything from cars to chainsaws ... and they're still used today.

Robotting into the future

Since Victor built his arm, robotics has gone from strength to strength. You can buy robots that vacuum your floor, mow your lawn or carry your golf clubs. There are emotion-reading robots for the lonely, pet robots for those living in a no-pets house, and swarming robots that work as individuals or join forces to form a larger robot. There are even self-sustaining EcoBots that power themselves by eating flies (and they're rather efficient: eight flies can last twelve days). Mind. Blown.

Plus, we have surgical robots for operating on humans, entertainer robots for entertaining humans, rescue robots for rescuing humans, and humanoid robots for … acting like humans?

And that is just the beginning. We have robots for helping people re-learn how to walk, robots for teaching gym classes, and even robots for going to school if you're sick and stuck at home.

Machine learning

If you want a computer to know the difference between an apple and a pear, you can teach it. It's as simple as showing it thousands of pictures of apples, labelled 'apple', and thousands of pictures of pears, labelled 'pear'.

The computer then uses these experiences to learn—all by itself—which combinations of pixels are likely to be a pear, and which are likely to be an apple.

This is incredibly useful if you're selecting a bowl of fruit. But fruit-spotting isn't all machines can do.

Machine learning lets computers discover cheats, diagnose

illness, sort spam, recommend TV shows, or match a Snapchat filter to your face. And that's only the beginning.

Do you need a hand?

Robots are helping humans, big time. And we invented them to be helpful, so yay.

But at what point does helpful become too helpful? We've invented an AI babysitter that records what kids do, teaches them good manners, and says caring things to them when they're crying. But don't let that freak you out. It looks like a box. Okay. Now you can freak out.

Meanwhile, we're creating humanoid robots that are self-aware, feel emotion, have amazing hair (jealous much?), and can chat for hours about everything from favourite movies to recipes for concrete.

AI bots can also write stories, paint pictures and compose music. They can even write fake news. One example is food reviewing: They simply analyse millions of online food reviews, then use what they've learned to write and post their own reviews, even though they're computer programs and have never ever eaten anything. Not even concrete.

Keeping an eye on AI

Squillionaire inventor Elon Musk is big into technology. You may know him from SpaceX, Tesla Motors, Hyperloop, OpenAI, Neuralink, SolarCity and whatever he dreams up next.

But Elon knows that technology is only as good as the people who use it. The technology in driverless cars helps them avoid crashing into humans. But that technology can also be used in driverless weapons to help them crash into humans.

That's why Elon, along with loads of other AI experts, wrote a letter to the United Nations. The letter asked that AI research be focused on social good, and not evil.

'Because of the great potential of AI, it is important to research how to reap its benefits while avoiding potential pitfalls.' Open letter

'Our AI systems must do what we want them to do.' Open letter

Stuff robots can already do better:

- **Boring jobs**, like processing data, or noticing when something changes. Think watching for a supernova, or predicting the weather.
- **Dangerous jobs**, where humans might get splattered, radiated, sliced, exploded or otherwise separated from their lives. Think defusing bombs or surveying radioactive land.
- **Repetitive jobs**, where you need to do the same thing over and over. Think flipping hamburgers or laying bricks.
- **Complicated jobs**, where you need to think about heaps of variables before you decide on the right thing to do. Think diagnosing diseases based on patient databases.

- **Predictable jobs**, where you look at what has already happened to decide what you need to do next. Think robot lawyers that analyse past cases to predict the outcome in a new case.
- **Expensive jobs,** where you need to pay a whole lot of people to work on something. Instead, you could buy robots, and pay them nothing. Think slave robot army.
- **Things that are not jobs**, where you just want to enjoy your time and stretch your brain. Think chess, poker and even video games.

Stuff humans can do better:

- **Maybe being creative?** But computers are learning how to invent jokes and create storylines specifically designed to amuse or surprise humans.
- **Maybe feeling empathy?** But we're also designing robots to decipher human expressions and offer human comfort.
- Um ...?

Into the future

Ever heard of the robot apocalypse? It's when the uber-intelligent, super-high-tech robots of the world rise up to take humankind prisoner and rule the Earth. Some predictions involve an intelligent RoboNet, where millions of robots are connected via the internet to share their intelligence, their observations and their will to dominate the universe.

Of course, this hasn't yet happened. Perhaps it never will. But as we make computers faster and smarter, maybe keeping them under control is something we should consider.

```
USER Sophia, an AI humanoid robot

PRINT.STRING 'In the future, I hope to do
    things such as go to school, study,
    make art, start a business, even
    have my own home and family, but
    I am not considered a legal person
    and cannot yet do these things.'
```

'Do you want to destroy humans? Please say no.'
David Hanson, creator of Sophia

```
USER Sophia

PRINT.STRING 'OK. I will destroy humans.'
```

What would you do?

- Say you're programming a driverless car. In a dangerous situation, the car's AI will need to act fast, to avoid a crash. But there's a bicycle on the road. And another car. And you can't avoid them all. Do you crash into the car to save the cyclist? Or do you crash into the bike to avoid the car? What if the car was a truck? What if the bike was a pram?
- If you could create a robot to help with some part of your life, what would it be? Plan a story with your robot in it. How many ways could your story end? What actions are key to achieving a happy ending?
- Design and label a robot you'd love to own. What are its key features? How is it powered?

Quantum computing, augmented reality and ... whatever comes next

These last 200 years have been a pretty packed ride. A lot has changed since Charles made his cow-catcher, and since Sophie built her cow-feeder. Now we have cow-milking robots, cow-herding robots, cow-milking apps for your mobile, and cow-shaped walking robots for the military. And that's just the cows.

So what's next?

The tech: The combined computing fruits from decades of human achievement
Controlled by: You

Would you rather?

Thanks to centuries of human invention, you have the wildest tech-tools at your disposal. Yes, you. So what are you going to do with all this power?

Research suggests you're so used to online friending, you've forgotten how to make real friends. That you're so used to texting, you can no longer have a real-life conversation. That you're not interested in the real world, because you have a virtual world at your fingertips, all from the comfort of your couch.

'Man will become a passive, purposeless, machine-conditioned animal.' Lewis Mumford, *The Myth of the Machine*, 1970

Other research suggests you're grabbing life with both hands: using technology to become more engaged and active in the community, using computers to form networks and create change. That you know what you want the future to look like, and you're playing a part in taking us there.

Your brain

If your brain was a computer, it'd have more than 3500 terabytes of memory and a speed of 38 thousand trillion operations per second. Even so, some people think computers will be smarter than humans by 2045.

It's a cat's life

Elon Musk once said that if robots start doing everything for us, we risk becoming 'house cats' in our own home. He thinks the key to staying smarter than computers is a brain–machine interface called neural lace. The idea is, you stick it inside your skull, and you use it like an old-fashioned mouse. Yep.

Elon's not the only one gunning for a future without keyboards and wires. The future may bring computers you control with the wave of a hand, or the blink of an eye.

Tech tatts and injectables

We've been wearing computers for a while: think Fitbits and smart watches. So why not go the extra mile? Researchers are looking into smart sensors you inject under your skin, tattoos that provide information, T-shirts that let you feel the hits you take in a computer game ...

VR, AR and WT?

Technology has changed the world, and it's also changing how we see the world ... Take virtual reality, for example.

Simply stick on a headset, and you feel as if you're in a whole new world. You might be sitting in your bedroom, but what you see and hear and feel can trick your brain into thinking you're fighting aliens in another solar system, for example (even though you know you're not).

Augmented reality may be even cooler. Look through your phone or tablet, and you'll see new dimensions in your real world: the tech adds to or slightly changes your environment. You might be sitting in your bedroom, but what you see and hear and feel can trick your brain into thinking there's an alien sitting next to you on your bed—and worse, it's hogging your doona.

Augmented reality also helps you better understand your environment. Google Lens, for example, crunches data on everything it sees. It works out (and offers advice on) what you're looking at, where you are, and what you might like to do while you're there.

- Great pizza place across the road.
- Bougainvillea might need pruning.
- Hit the deck! Low-flying plane!

The new rubbish

Because technology is always improving, tech companies release new hardware all the time: That new phone feeling. That new laptop feeling. That new printer feeling. That new sinking feeling when you look in your garage and see a whole stack of defunct electronic goods. Because what happens to all that old stuff? Museum? Paperweight? Landfilled and leaching toxins?

Your old electronics are the world's new e-waste. And guess what? We produce millions of tonnes of e-waste every year. Much of it can be recycled—the metals, plastic, wiring. But many of the resources that go into making new electronics can be toxic, including poisonous metals such as lead, mercury, cadmium and even arsenic. Plus it's expensive to recycle e-waste safely. In many places, e-waste is recycled without health regulations. In others, it's just popped into landfill. What happened to your family's old TV, laptop or outdated phone?

Surfing the quantum wave

Just as we made the switch from mechanical computers to electronic computers, we might one day graduate to quantum computers. Quantum computing relies on minier-than-microscopic subatomic particles. And when you start working with things this tiny, all the rules go out the window.

If you recall, binary computers rely on transistors switching on (1) and off (0). Each 1 or 0 is called a 'bit'. Repeat for a few billion 'bits', and you have a computer.

But instead of bits, quantum computers have 'qubits'. A bit can only be a 0 or a 1, but a qubit can be pretty much whatever it wants. It can be 0, 1, 0 and 1 at the same time, or something in between. Confused? See above: all the rules go out the window.

This means that, theoretically, a quantum computer could do multiple operations simultaneously. Which means, theoretically, it could work fast enough to leave electronic computers for dust.

Qu-baby steps

So far quantum computing is taking baby steps. For example, US researcher Isaac Chuang used laser pulses to create a 5-qubit computer using five atoms. IBM released a 16-qubit processor, making it freely available for developers and researchers to ~~play with~~ work on.

'In future generations, we foresee it being straightforwardly scalable, once the apparatus can trap more atoms and more laser beams can control the pulses.' Isaac Chuang

Some estimates say that a workable quantum computer could be just ten years away. Want to help make it?

'All you have to do is go in the lab, apply more technology, and you should be able to make a bigger quantum computer.' Isaac Chuang

Into the future

Well, this is embarrassing. I don't really know what to write here. I mean, the future hasn't happened yet. This is as far as we've gone.

But since you've come this far, I wonder ... Could you lend me a hand? Take a moment or two, stir in what you know and add a dash of what you dream, and imagine the future.

I imagine the future gets better and better. Because most of us are good people and we want more good in our world.

The future won't happen overnight. Well, not all of it, anyway.

But we can at least get that party started.

What will you do?

This is your bit. It's entirely your choice. This is the world you live in, the ball of rock and ocean on which you will grow up. So how do you want to spend your time? What do you want your world to look like? What you choose to do with your days can change the way we live. All you need is imagination, innovation and a bit of hard work.

And pizza. That seems to be quite key.

Bye!
:-)